Safe
AND
Secure

PLANNED LIFETIME ADVOCACY NETWORK (PLAN)

The strategies offered in this book are provided for the general guidance and benefit of the reader. This book provides information. It does not provide legal advice.

The information contained in the book is accurate at the date of publishing. However, we recommend that readers contact their own professional advisor or consultant when planning to implement any strategies. This will ensure the latest available information is taken into consideration and matched with the individual's or family's circumstances.

 PLAN – Planned Lifetime Advocacy Network
101B - 3790 Canada Way
Burnaby B.C. V5G 1G4
Phone   604 439-9566
Fax   604 439-7001
Toll-free: 1-888-696-7526
Web site: http://www.planbcteladvanced.com

This workbook uses the term "disability" to refer to those challenges, conditions, circumstances, handicaps, and impairments that limit the functional ability of people. As is common in most publications of this kind, the person is the focus, the disability secondary.

Canadian Cataloguing in Publication Data
Etmanski, Al, 1947-
Safe and secure

ISBN 0-9680462-0-7

1. Handicapped – Family relationships.   2. Handicapped – Finance, Personal.   3. Estate planning.   I. Collins, Jack, 1929-   II. Cammack, Vickie, 1951-   III. Planned Lifetime Advocacy Network.   IV. Title

HV1568.E85 1995   362.4'043   C95-911060-7

Design and production by Working Design

Safe AND Secure

SIX STEPS TO CREATING A
PERSONAL FUTURE PLAN FOR
PEOPLE WITH DISABILITIES

Al Etmanski
with Jack Collins & Vickie Cammack

PLANNED LIFETIME ADVOCACY NETWORK (PLAN)
REVISED EDITION 1997

To Our Children –
All of Them

Acknowledgments

The contents of this book are mined from ten years of persistence, caring and creativity from a group of remarkable families – the founding Board members of PLAN: Jack Collins, Dick McCallum, Joan Lawrence, Chuck Walker, Duncan McEwen, Gloria Roberts, Ron Duff, Ernie Bryan and Anne Saen. Cathy Herb-Kelly, Mary Hamilton, Gerry Hodgson, Christine Gordon, Cathy Anthony, Sharon Miles, Sharon DiSanto, Marty Wittman and Arthur Mudry provided invaluable encouragement and critical feedback. They discovered gems we never knew existed.

Davis & Company provided the information upon which our Will Planning Worksheet in Step 5 is based.

Gayla Reid took our rough diamond and polished it to a high shine as editor.

The Law Foundation, particularly Jane McFadgen, invested in our dream long before anyone else and tolerated every one of our struggles with the muse.

Finally to my co-authors, love had everything to do with it. We have ventured further than anyone ever thought possible.

FUNDING GENEROUSLY PROVIDED BY

THE LAW FOUNDATION OF BRITISH COLUMBIA

VanCity Community Foundation

Contents

The Steps

Worksheets

Appendix

Assisting families to create a secure future

Ring the bells that
still can ring
Forget your
perfect offering
There is a crack
in everything
That's how the
light gets in.
LEONARD COHEN

This book has been inspired by parents and families who, like you, have sons and daughters, or brothers and sisters with disabilities. Regardless of our relatives' ages, our concerns are the same. Who will take an interest in them when we are gone? Who will give them love? Who will protect them and see that they are safe?

The answers to those questions led a small but energetic group of parents in British Columbia to create a new organization, Planned Lifetime Advocacy Network (PLAN). PLAN was established in 1989, after four years of research by a group of older parents who called themselves the Senior Parents Network. PLAN is the first and only Canadian organization offering a full range of advice and assistance on future planning.

PLAN exists for one main reason – to assist families create a secure future for their children with disabilities. PLAN offers:
- a lifetime commitment to monitor the quality of life once the parents/family die
- information and referral on all future planning issues
- assistance with will and estate planning
- workshops
- a quarterly newsletter
- parent-to-parent support and consultation
- family meetings
- help in developing Personal Networks of support
- advice on home ownership
- information on government benefits
- a voice to government about the concerns of parents
- alternatives to guardianship

At PLAN, we are finally self-sufficient. If we were not, we would have to become reliant on government. An arms-length relationship from government is what enables us to effectively monitor, advocate, and protect the best interests of people with disabilities.

We have learned a lot in the past ten years. We've survived without government funding, which is quite an achievement. And our membership has grown rapidly. Enquiries come from all over Canada and are starting to trickle in from the United States.

We now want to share what we've learned with as many families as possible. So please use this book. It's been developed with love. Begin the process. Adapt it to meet your needs. Action, as the philosopher Goethe said, has boldness, magic, and genius in it.

Jack Collins
FOUNDING PRESIDENT, PLAN

Love is not enough

Our purpose

1. To inspire you to develop a Personal Future Plan.

2. To guide you through our process.

3. To offer practical tips and technical advice.

There are at least two emotions that inspired you to pick up this book. The first is love. The second is fear. We know this because we experience them too, as do the hundreds of parents of children with disabilities we have met over the years. You are definitely not alone.

Like everyone else, you want to die with your affairs in order. You want to leave a clear blueprint of your wishes for your loved ones. At a time of great emotional stress – your death – you want to minimize the trauma. You also want to provide a secure future for those who survive you, particularly your son or daughter with a disability.

That's the voice of love speaking.

Nevertheless, over 50 per cent of Canadians die without a will. Most of the other 50 per cent haven't had their will reviewed and updated for at least five years. And surprisingly, over 90 per cent of all business owners in North America die without a viable estate plan. From our own experience at Planned Lifetime Advocacy Network, less than 5 per cent of the thousands of people who have attended a PLAN workshop on wills and estates actually complete and execute their will.

That's the voice of fear speaking.

So let's get right down to it. In matters of future planning, love is not enough. That's one of the main reasons this book has been written. We want to do three things:

1. We want to motivate, inspire and challenge you:
- to begin and complete the future planning process for your loved one
- to conquer your fears
- to replace fear of the future with faith in the future

2. We want to guide you through the process of creating a

"Personal Future Plan" for your relative with a disability. We want to expand your vision of the possibilities and to help you put them into concrete terms.

3. Finally, we want to shed light on the legal/financial/technical solutions available to assist you to carry out your last wishes, and to share practical tips on how to apply these solutions to your unique circumstances.

What we believe

> My soul, do not aspire to immortal life, but cultivate those fields that are possible.
>
> PINDAR,
> 5TH CENTURY B.C.

We believe in families. We believe in your initiative, your dedication, your creativity, your tenacity and your commitment. We believe that your wishes, dreams and desires for your loved one can shape the future. We believe in a world of possibilities. We believe that if you are willing to commit to the process of future planning outlined in this workbook, then that is the future your loved one will have.

This book allows you to look over the shoulders of families like yours. In this workbook, you will meet people who are breathing life into their dreams right now and giving shape to a brighter future for themselves and for their loved ones with disabilities. While the details of their plans may be different, the issues they are confronting are remarkably similar to yours.

Another belief of ours is that this book can help. It will provide you with an overview of the whole future planning process. There are no single answers, no single solutions, no miracles. In fact, some of the solutions will never look perfect. A Personal Future Plan is just a mixture of old-fashioned common sense, commitment, hard work, and a dash of bravado.

So enjoy, create, laugh and cry.

Developing a Personal Future Plan – Six steps to a safe and secure future

Many of us never really take the time to sit down and discuss what our future intentions are for our loved one with a

How to use this book

We suggest you skim through this book until you come to a section you'd like to work on. Once you've decided to focus on one section, answer all the questions and complete all the worksheets. You'll be surprised how the questions in one section will lead directly into the concerns of another section. Each one informs and guides the other. Before you know it, your planning will be complete and you'll have a complete record of your intentions – all contained in this book.

This book will allow you to be an informed consumer of the professional services that are available in the future planning industry. By following the steps and advice presented here, you will be better prepared, use less professional time, and save yourself money.

We invite you to customize this book to your needs. Add your own personal data, photos, records, medical information, etc. Keep it in a safe place. You should never underestimate how valuable this information will be to your survivors someday. Think of it as your manuscript to the future.

disability. Nevertheless it does come up. Maybe it pops up when you are driving home from a family gathering. Maybe one of your children mentions something in passing, but the topic quickly changes. Maybe you wake up in the middle of the night and decide it's time to talk about it in the morning. But then you don't.

So many thoughts, ideas, worries and concerns go rolling around in your head. You can hardly remember them all. How could you expect someone else to? There are so many confusing messages and countless pieces of advice, and so many complications. The need for resolution lurks just beneath the surface, emerging at the most unexpected times.

Sound familiar? That's our experience, too. Virtually all of the families we have worked with have encountered the seemingly overwhelming bits and pieces of advice and action required to prepare for the future.

Our work with families over the past ten years has convinced us that the process is not as complicated as it first appears. Further, we are convinced there are only a few key elements you need to focus on. We have combined these elements into what we call a Personal Future Plan. That is what this book is about. It is what we advise you to develop for your loved one. But really, you will be developing it for yourself.

A Personal Future Plan is a six-step process families can follow to create a safe, secure, and pleasant future for their family members with disabilities. It includes the best of your experiences, your dreams and nightmares, your wishes for the future, and your knowledge and expertise. It combines all of these with the active involvement of your loved one with a disability, other members of your family, and selected knowledgeable professionals.

It is a plan that you create, control, and direct. It is focused on the here and now. It is also geared to a time when you will no longer be around.

The six steps are as follows:

STEP ONE	**Clarifying Your Vision**
STEP TWO	**Building Relationships**
STEP THREE	**Controlling the Home Environment**
STEP FOUR	**Preparing for Decision-Making**
STEP FIVE	**Developing Your Will and Estate Plan**
STEP SIX	**Securing Your Plan**

Clarifying *your* Vision

Whatever you can do,
or dream you can, begin it.
Boldness has genius,
power and magic in it.

GOETHE

Rick's chances were down to one

GEORGE HALL'S life is a paradox. Like that popular movie of the eighties, George has gone "back to the future."

"My wife and I always felt we should be independent with this problem," says George. "Yet seven months before she died my wife said, 'We still haven't done anything about Rick.'"

George's story is a familiar one to parents raising children with disabilities just after the Second World War.

"After Rick's birth, my wife and I, well mainly my wife, focused our time and energies raising Rick. There wasn't an infant development program then, you know. A bunch of us parents got together. We helped each other. We started a school for Rick and others like him in the basement of one of the local churches. Nothing fancy, mind you. And we raised the money to hire the teachers and buy the supplies. Eventually we got the government to take them over.

"I was involved in the local association from 1961 to 1971. For a time I was on the provincial board as well.

"I remember back in the seventies, someone proposed a Lifetime Friendship Plan. The idea was to pay for friends to look in on the disabled person after their parents died. You see, parents were always concerned about their child's future. We used to talk about it all the time. What would happen if one or both of us were run over by a car? I used to phone the provincial association periodically to see if there were any new developments. There never were.

"Then my wife took ill and matters really came to a head. We did have our will prepared during that time and we arranged with a trust company to manage the money we left in Rick's trust.

"Still my wife kept saying, 'Isn't there something else we can do?'"

After George's wife died, he was devastated. "As you can imagine it was a terribly painful time. Normally I'm a pretty optimistic person but I confess there were days when my dreams for Rick turned into nightmares.

"I knew I had to do something. Somehow the plans my wife and I had put in place didn't seem adequate now that she was gone. I figured Rick's chances were down to one."

•

This haunted George. Finally in March 1988 he made one of his periodic calls to the provincial association. This time they had an answer. They mentioned the Senior Parents Network and suggested he might want to look into it. The Senior Parents Network was simply a group of parents in similar situations. Their common bond was their willingness to search for an answer to this question: "If we were to die tomorrow, what would happen to our mentally handicapped child?"

George found an instant solidarity with these parents. Their worries were the same as his. Their questions were no

continued on page 18

Clarifying Your Vision

Our convictions

There is a future.

•

Whatever you decide can be changed.

•

You will proceed faster by starting than by stalling.

•

An imperfect plan is better than no plan at all.

•

Family and friends are the heart of the matter.

•

Money, trusts, and wills are simply vehicles.

•

Safety and happiness for your loved one is the goal.

•

You won't run out of gas.

Remember the old saying: If you don't know where you are going, any road will get you there? Well, we think it's true. That's why, as you begin your Personal Future Plan, you need to be clear about what you want. What are you trying to achieve for your child or relative? What are your goals? What do you want to prevent? To maintain? What do you want people to know when they gather around to discuss your wishes after you have gone?

Without clear answers to these questions, the rest of your planning will be cloudy and incomplete. Knowing what you want to achieve is the first step to creating a Personal Future Plan.

We have found that families embarking on this process think they should first be paying attention to the technical solutions. In reality, ninety per cent of the planning time should be spent identifying what you are trying to achieve, thinking through your goals and objectives, and clarifying your vision. Once these are clear, you will be in a better position to evaluate the various options available. Then the technical solutions, such as increasing the value of your estate, choosing your trustee, and finding the precise legal clauses, will follow. Then, and only then, should you seek the advice of professionals.

Think of your last plane ride. Did you ask the pilot where you should go? Of course not. You made that decision first. Then you examined the options available to you around scheduling, service, price, and so on. That's the most effective way to utilize the services of professionals in the future planning business. The good ones will give you the same advice. It saves them time and you money.

different from the ones on his mind.

George liked their honesty. He enjoyed their candour and humour. They were in league together. Parents helping parents.

That motivation led this group of senior parents to mount an international search to discover how parents elsewhere were confronting the challenge of creating a secure future for people with disabilities. They collected material from Canada, United States, Australia, New Zealand and England.

They discovered that conditions for people with disabilities were universal. Institutions were closing. Government financial support for services was either in decline or threatened. Health care was being rationed in some areas. Formal monitoring was non-existent in most places. Services and programs had their limitations. They didn't provide many opportunities for friendship. Many people with disabilities remained lonely and isolated.

In response, parents elsewhere had begun to create advocacy trusts or continuity foundations. These were usually family financed and directed, non-profit organizations. They were dedicated to protecting the quality of life of people with disabilities after their parents became infirm or died. George and the others took the best of what existed elsewhere and spent the next five years developing the Planned Lifetime Advocacy Network (PLAN) organization.

George was so impressed by the thoroughness of the review that he became a founding board member of PLAN. He agreed with their philosophy – self-sufficiency through member contributions, entrepreneurial fund raising, and independence from government. As parents who had been promised many miracles during the life of their child with a disability, they were careful not to promise any miracles.

They had two assets. One was their wisdom. They liked to joke that their past mistakes had created enough scar tissue to make them clever. Now they had good instincts. They could smell the mistakes coming around the second time. Their second asset was the interest and enthusiasm of a younger generation of parents. By this time the Senior Parents Network had become a full-fledged society, PLAN, open to parents of all ages. The generation gap that has the potential to divide had been bridged.

As George said, "I had always felt a bit uncomfortable with the younger parents I met. They seemed so naive. I felt they were in for the same big surprise we experienced when our kids got older. Most people think kids are cute and want to help, but they fall by the wayside as our kids become adults. And I suppose they saw me as an old fuddy-duddy. But we have so much in common. PLAN has given us the opportunity to work together. With their energy and our wisdom no one can stop us now." ■

Worksheets

Three worksheets are located at the end of this chapter, starting on page 24. Take a look at them now, and plan to fill them out when you're ready to begin developing your Personal Future Plan.

Worksheet 1 – After You're Gone: Clarifying Your Vision provides you with a list of questions you can use to get started.

Worksheet 2 – A Family Portrait provides an important record of your loved one's family experiences.

Worksheet 3 – A Letter to the Future should contain what you would like to see happen in the future. If writing isn't your cup of tea, get out a tape recorder or videotape and dictate your letter to the future.

What is a vision?

Visions are creations of the heart as well as of the head. A vision is your description of a desired future for your child or relative. A vision is about passion – your passion for the future security of your loved one. That's why it's so important to address the dreams as well as the nightmares.

A clear statement of your vision will help focus your attention. Since a vision reflects your values, your traditions, and your family history, it creates a personality for the other components of your Personal Future Plan.

Clarify your vision before you seek technical help.

Clarifying your vision:
- allows you to see the results
- encourages you to involve other members of the family
- allows others who become involved with your loved one to better understand what's at stake
- helps you discriminate between preferred and undesirable results
- suggests new opportunities
- paves a pathway for moving forward
- provides a basis for people (including other family members) to rally around

How often have we been told by a mom that her other children know the complete medical background of her son, only to find that they were too busy growing up to notice, let alone make notes! How often has a dad told us that he intends to rely on his next-door neighbours to carry out his wishes for his daughter, and then it turns out he has never discussed any details with them!

So what are we afraid of?

Before we go any further, we need to talk about why so many people don't prepare adequately for the future. What keeps so many of us from formalizing our future wishes for our survivors? What causes our paralysis? Why don't we act? Fear.

Love and fear are two sides of the same coin. The coin is called passion. The word, passion, stems from the Greek and Latin words for suffering. Wouldn't you agree that suffering is a mixture of love and fear?

Fear is an intriguing emotion. Fear distorts our perception and confuses us about what is going on and about what is possible. When, for example, we use words like *can't, ought to, if only, doubt,* and *impossible,* we are under the influence of fear. Fear draws a dark and cold curtain between our intentions and our actions. Like a school-yard bully, its appearance is deceiving. It's more imposing in our minds than in reality.

In our own personal struggles with the issues of future planning and in our work with families, we can identify three "school-yard bullies" that everyone must summon the courage to confront. We offer them here because we believe that where there is clarity, there is comfort. Where there is understanding, there is the ability to change.

FEAR OF OPENING UP Creating a future plan means discussing intensely personal and private matters with others – with family members, friends or acquaintances, and professionals. We may need to contact people who, we feel, are not interested in our loved one. Or we may not know which professionals to turn to or trust.

We've grown up believing in self-sufficiency. We've taken our responsibilities seriously. We've done the best we can. We've tried all our lives to make sure others wouldn't have to

> It is not because things are difficult that we do not dare; it is because we do not dare that they are difficult.
> SENECA

shoulder our responsibilities.

With future planning we have to share our hopes, our dreams, our fears and anxieties with others:

- We need to ask others to help us with our planning.
- We need to ask others to carry out our wishes after we are gone.
- We need to be able to share our children, and trust others to believe in our children's possibilities for the future.

To do this, we need to reach out. We need to know who we can rely on. After all, what good are your plans if no one else knows about them? Sure, they could read about your wishes in your will. But will the readers get the complete picture? Will they know what you really want? What if they have questions? How can you be sure you will be understood?

FEAR OF DEATH Death is not a popular topic in our society. Even a cursory look at the popular media suggests that our culture is obsessed with youth, living forever, and avoiding sickness and infirmity. An illusion is offered: we can cheat death. While it may not be stated, the implicit message is that diet, exercise, and medical intervention will keep us "forever young" or "forever alive." As Margaret Mead said, "When people are born we rejoice, and when they're married we celebrate, but when they die we try to pretend nothing has happened."

The fear of death is there for all of us. It lurks just beneath the surface, never deep enough to be quite ignored. Perhaps it presents as anxiety, perhaps as an awful sense of impermanence, perhaps as loneliness. We may harbour the utopian belief that others have fewer anxieties about death than we do. But all of us are affected by the image of our death. Perhaps what divides us is not so much being exempt from this fear, but living with the knowledge and going forward in spite of our fears.

For younger parents in particular, death can feel very remote. Even thinking about it can seem a kind of perversity. But death is a natural part of life which we all have to face sooner or later, and which we cannot overcome. The Dalai Lama says there are two ways we can choose to deal with the prospect of our death: we can ignore it or we can confront it. By thinking clearly about death, we can try to minimize the suffering our death may bring.

FEAR OF MAKING A MISTAKE, OF NOT BEING PERFECT Now here's an irony for you. In thinking about the future, many of us feel we need to create the perfect plan. We are afraid that we haven't covered all the bases. Somehow we think we can control the future even though we struggle to negotiate the day-to-day.

According to financial and estate planners, lawyers, and everyone else involved in the future planning business, the most common excuse for not making a will is the fear of not getting it right. Indecision can paralyze those with the best intentions. Perfection equals postponement. In trying to make perfect decisions, we risk indefinite delay.

> He has half the deed done who has made a beginning.
> HORACE

Plans evolve

Future plans will change as circumstances change. It takes time for our dreams to evolve. You can always update and revise your future plan. In fact, you should expect to make changes as life carries on and as you pick up tips here and there. Who among us can predict the future? Can we anticipate all eventualities?

Top ten reasons for not preparing for your future

1. The future is uncertain. Better eat dessert first. SARAH LEE
2. I'm afraid that if I make a will, I will die. JOE AVERAGE
3. There's no shame in avoiding elephants. VIETNAMESE PROVERB
4. I'll get to it as soon as I finish this one little chore. GOLIATH, PHILISTINE GIANT, 1013 B.C.
5. I'm not afraid to die. I just don't want to be there when it happens. WOODY ALLEN
6. I don't see any dark clouds on the horizon. There's nothing to worry about. GENERAL CUSTER, U.S. CAVALRY
7. I've developed a new philosophy – I only dread one day at a time. CHARLES M. SCHULZ, PEANUTS
8. Dying is a very dull and dreary affair. I intend to have nothing to do with it. SOMERSET MAUGHAM
9. I trust the government.
10. Only a few years to the year 2020.

Here's a simple exercise: Place yourself twenty years in the past. Who would have predicted the breakup of the Soviet Union? The destruction of the Berlin Wall? The career of your children? The amount of your savings?

To put it another way: Have you ever made a decision without having all the answers? Would Columbus have set sail? Would Mother Theresa have moved to the slums of Calcutta? The truth is that we often have to proceed as best we can without all the answers. Hindsight is the only guarantee of perfect vision. ■

Putting it off

- We're not in crisis yet. We've still got lots of time.
- The process is too costly both financially and emotionally.
- I don't know who to turn to. My community of support is too small,
- I'm worn out from too many previous battles. I just need a break.
- We're still young.
- The future is too hard to contemplate.
- I'm a procrastinator. What more can I say?

Having a Personal Future Plan

- It's fair to other family members. They now know what's going on.
- I'm relieved. That's a load off my shoulders.
- My worries about government interference are gone.
- I'm better prepared to face the unknown.
- I've done the best I can.
- I've left a legacy of love.
- I'm at peace.

Worksheet 1

AFTER YOU'RE GONE: CLARIFYING YOUR VISION

It's the day after your death. Describe what a safe and secure life will look like for

your loved one from now on. _____

_____

_____

_____

_____

List ten words to describe a typical day for your loved one, in the best of all possible

worlds. _____

_____

_____

_____

Use some key words to describe your worst nightmare for your loved one after

you're gone. _____

_____

What is the most important message you want to leave your loved one?

_____

_____

_____

What do you want your other surviving family members to help with after you've

gone? _____

_____

_____

When your executors/trustees meet, what do you want them to do first?

_____

_____

_____

What are the three priorities you want future care-givers to remember about your

loved one?

1. _____

2. _____

3. _____

What are the important arrangements you've made to ensure quality of life for your

loved one? _____

_____

_____

_____

_____

How do you want to be remembered by your loved one?

_____

_____

_____

Worksheet 2

A FAMILY PORTRAIT

Use this worksheet to develop a portrait of your loved one. It will be an important record to pass on to your survivors. This is a lengthy worksheet; we suggest you complete it in your own time. Give yourself an opportunity to reflect on all of the issues.

Health

List names of current doctors, specialists and health practitioners:

_____

_____

_____

List current health concerns: _____

_____

_____

_____

List current health treatments: _____

_____

_____

_____

List current health precautions and alternatives: _____

_____

_____

_____

Briefly describe key features of medical history: _____

_____

_____

_____

Education and Work

List current educational and/or work activity: _____

_____

_____

_____

What are your future dreams in this area? What other possibilities would you like

to see explored? _____

_____

_____

What are some highlights from your child or relative's school experience? What did your loved one like about it? What didn't your loved one like about it? _____

_____

_____

_____

_____

Who are the people from the past that your loved one had or still has a close connection with? _____

_____

_____

_____

What are some highlights of your child or relative's work experience? What did your loved one like about it? What didn't your loved one like about it? _____

_____

_____

_____

_____

Housing

Describe current living arrangements: _____

_____

_____

_____

What are some future housing options/possibilities for your loved one?

_____

_____

_____

Summarize briefly previous living arrangements: _____

_____

_____

_____

What did your loved one like about them? Dislike about them? _____

_____

_____

_____

_____

Who are the people who had a significant relationship with your loved one in these previous living arrangements? _____

_____

_____

_____

Leisure and Recreation

List current social, recreational, cultural, artistic and athletic activities:

_____

_____

_____

_____

What are your loved one's interests and preferred activities in these areas?

_____

_____

_____

_____

What are some future possibilities in the area of leisure and recreation?

_____

_____

_____

What does your loved one most like to do? _____

_____

_____

_____

Personal

How would you describe your family's beliefs and values? _____

_____

_____

_____

What customs and traditions are important in your family? _____

_____

_____

_____

Is spiritual and religious worship important for your loved one? Is this an area that could be explored further? _____

_____

_____

What are the significant events, markers or milestones in your loved one's life?

_____

_____

_____

_____

What brings comfort and peace to your loved one? _____

_____

_____

_____

What has been your loved one's greatest source of emotional support?

_____

_____

_____

What does your loved one derive the most pleasure from? _____

_____

_____

_____

Who are the most significant people in your loved one's life? _____

_____

_____

_____

What are your loved one's favourite possessions? _____

_____

_____

_____

Worksheet 3

A LETTER TO THE FUTURE

The last wishes of parents for their children are honoured and respected in our society. A letter to the future is your opportunity to tell your survivors how you would like to be remembered, and how you would like your loved one with a disability to be loved and cared for.

This is not an easy letter to write. Think of it as the letter your might write in the middle of the night when you can't sleep. Be frank about your hopes and fears. Tell those who will survive you what's most important to you.

Dear _____,

_____

_____

_____

_____

_____

_____

_____

_____

_____

_____

With love,

Building Relationships

The bird a nest,
The spider a web,
Man friendship.
WILLIAM BLAKE

A web of support for Rick

"I USED TO WORK in government, you know. In government they come up with all kinds of programs. Many of them are baloney – no matter how thin you slice it! At one of these senior parent meetings, this young woman came around and started talking about circles – circles of friends. Well, I have to admit I thought it was one of those baloney stories. How could this possibly work?

"It was too theoretical. It looked good on paper but it would never work. I thought it was all gobbledygook.

"But they turned the tables on me. They said they wanted a guinea pig for one of those circle things. I guess they figured if they could convince me they could convince anyone. Several of the other parents were prepared to take the risk. So I took a chance. Remembering what my wife had asked I said to myself, 'What have I got to lose?'

"Now, at the time Rick knew only a couple of people. He had a very narrow social life. He bowled once a week. And he attended a program at the community centre. That was it. He wasn't working or in any kind of a day program at the time although he used to work at Campbell Industries."

When George came home to talk to Rick about the circle, he got a chilly reception. In fact, Rick was downright cold to the idea. Rick was emphatic. He wouldn't have anything to do with the circle.

"Dad, you can have what you want. Just don't include me!" said Rick.

Not a great start.

George explains Rick's disinterest simply. "Rick had been to many meeting over the years and attended lots of classes and nothing ever changed for him. I guess I really couldn't blame him."

Despite his own ambivalence, George persevered. To this day he doesn't really know why. Perhaps it was the memory of his wife's insistence to do more. Perhaps it was his apprehension about the future – he was ready to try anything. Perhaps it was the assurance he felt from the other families who also were stepping into the unknown by forming circles.

There were lots of reasons why George should have been as firm as Rick in refusing to explore the "circle idea," as he still calls it. He and his wife had never discussed their concerns about Rick's future with any of their relatives. It was a private matter. Their responsibility and theirs alone. Who would be at all interested? Wouldn't they be too busy? Did they even like Rick?

George didn't know it at the time but this is the hardest part for most families – asking family and friends for help.

"It was the most awkward part of it," he admits. "You feel so exposed. You're brought up to take care of your own. Asking for help was just not in our vocabulary."

continued on page 40

Building Relationships

No one will ever be able to look after your child with the same persistence, interest, and determination as you do as a parent. That's a fact. However, unless you've tapped into the fountain of youth, you won't be around forever. That's a fact, too. So what's the next best thing? The answer is obvious. The best guarantee of a safe and secure future for a person with a disability is the number of caring, committed friends, family members, acquaintances and supporters actively involved in his or her life. It's as simple as that.

The real strength of these relationships comes not just in their connection to the person with a disability but in their connections with each other. Imagine a spider's web. The strands extend from the centre of the web to the edge. Imagine if there was nothing else holding them together. They would flap in the wind. Their functional value would be minimal. They need to be linked with each other to form the web. Otherwise spiders would starve! The strength of the web comes when all components are interconnected.

> *If I don't have friends, then I ain't got nothing.*
> BILLIE HOLIDAY

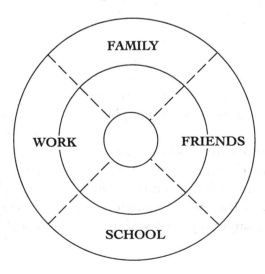

Finally he hit upon a solution. PLAN had developed a short questionnaire on examining the relationships in a person with a disability's life. George found the questions quite thought-provoking. He decided to mail the questions out to his relatives. His reasoning was simple. "I told them I was thinking about starting something like this for Rick. I figured this might be a way to test who might be receptive to the idea of a circle. If anybody showed any interest in Rick as a result of this, I would invite them to a meeting."

George also talked to a neighbour across the street who had always been friendly towards Rick. He invited this neighbour to the first meeting. He also invited a former staff person from the local association who would occasionally drop by to visit Rick.

"Anyway, so there we were, all of us sitting around the room talking about Rick. There were eight of us at the first meeting. Rick was in the other room, but his name kept coming up. I guess he was straining to listen. Pretty soon he was standing at the entrance to the living room. Before you knew it he was sitting down with the rest of us and joining in the conversation. That was a turning point for Rick and me. Neither of us could believe that people were actually interested in him that way.

"After the circle formed, Rick went through a change. He had always been very quiet – a bit of a loner. Either keeping to himself or doing things just with me. Never one to initiate a conversation. Never one to pick up the phone. Soon he found there were people he could talk to. And they would phone him. And they'd go for coffee or something. And he was phoning them!

"You know it all adds up. Rick gets all kinds of help now, beyond our wildest imagination. In fact I couldn't have imagined any of this five years ago."

For George that has been the greatest benefit of the "circle." He can sit back and watch a web of support being spun for Rick before his eyes. It's almost like watching a movie about the future from the comfort of your easy chair. George is confident that Rick's network isn't going to evaporate. He knows it doesn't depend solely on his input anymore. It will carry on without him. ■

It's the same for people. The focus of support for people with disabilities must be not only on their individual relationships but also on the relationships among their friends and supporters. These interconnections create the web of support that begins to approximate the thoroughness with which families care for each other.

The role of friendship in our lives

Some of our oldest literature attests to the importance of friendship in our lives. The Old Testament draws its lessons from tales about people and their relationships. These themes about our interconnectedness are but one indication that we are, above all else, social beings. Friendship is a necessity for all of us, as important and essential to life as food and drink.

Aristotle, a Greek philosopher and major influence on Western thought, put it succinctly: "For without friends no one would choose to live, though he had all other goods." Perhaps it's because friendship is so fundamental to our existence that we take it for granted, or we aren't conscious of its importance until it is brought to our attention.

A recent Canadian political leader's comment on his recovery from a life-threatening illness underscores this point. Aside from the centrality of his wife and children to his thoughts, he observed that much of his time during recuperation was spent counting the blessings of friendship. In particular, he recalled those friendships that had lapsed or been fractured and determined to repair them. Most of us, when asked to boil our life down to its basics, would likely have similar comments.

Nobody sees a flower, really. It is so small it takes time. We haven't time, and to see takes time, like having a friend takes time.
GEORGIA O'KEEFE

What the research says

- People with supportive social ties are less likely to become ill or die.

- Social contact reduces the likelihood of mental illness.

- Social supports contribute to the successful adjustment and well-being of the individual.

- Social supports affect the sense of control we have over our well-being and improves our ability to stick with healthy behaviour patterns.

- There is no label or attribute that prevents committed relationships from forming.

- Friendship aids the workings of the immune system.

We are *interdependent* not *independent* creatures and the impact of this recognition is far greater than our contemporary society appreciates or acknowledges. Understanding this interdependence is critical to our health, our quality of life, our sense of belonging, our peace of mind, and our security. And it is equally important to the future security of our sons and daughters with disabilities.

The essence of this future security is not the size of the estate we leave or how thorough the legal arrangements are. Yes, they are important factors in building a successful future plan for our relatives with disabilities. However, what completes the planning or makes it all worthwhile are social supports and relationships.

Friendships, ranging from acquaintances to intimate relationships, are formed by choice. They are freely given connections based on mutual interests. Friendships are reciprocal, a two-way exchange. They are not one-sided. The reasons for our connections with one another are varied. Similarly, there are a variety of ways to describe the functions of friendship. However, friendship usually involves:
- doing things with another person;
- doing things for another person; and
- sharing feelings or emotions.

The result of these exchanges is to create and reinforce the belief that we are valued. With social support we are more secure in our interdependence. The sense of being cared about by others reduces our loneliness, keeps us safe, enhances the quality of our life, and builds our sense of self-esteem.

A genuine friend is one who is faithful, devoted and true. We don't change ourselves to be with friends. Our gifts and our frailties are accepted as part of who we are. Our friends are not expected to fix us. They are just there. Friendships are naturally enjoyable.

The good feelings that arise from our connectedness to others are an obvious benefit of friendship. However, these are just the tip of the iceberg in evaluating the benefits of caring relationships. There is now a mass of evidence to indicate that such support may be one of the critical factors distinguishing those who remain healthy from those who fall ill. A review of the medical and health literature clearly indicates that social support is necessary for the maintenance of good health.

Relationships - a source of support

Think of our own lives. When our parents die, we are not alone. We are still surrounded by a circle of loved ones and friends. We want to create the same supportive experience for our child or relative with a disability. Reinforcing and building friendship is an attractive alternative for families worried about who will replace them when they are gone. The warmth, concern and caring that our friendships embody create a social environment of safety and security. And that spells comfort for moms and dads.

As the cycle of government support for people with disabilities begins to wane, we will have even stronger reasons for creating a buffer between welfare cutbacks and the welfare of our sons and daughters. And that's where the presence of friends and supporters becomes critical. Individuals who lack supportive ties are vulnerable to a wide variety of negative consequences. If you are not in the company of others, you may be at risk of abuse, neglect, and exploitation. People's needs can be jeopardized by the system's needs unless there are people around who care about the individual.

Let's be specific. Investing in an extended network of friends and family for our son or daughter provides both short-term and long-term returns.

Networks of personal support can serve as:
- monitors for the formal programs and services our loved ones receive
- companions
- advocates
- executor and trustee(s)
- resources for executors and trustees

Is a personal network useful for my loved one?

- Are there enough non-paid people in my loved one's life?

- Is there room for others to be involved?

- Am I anxious about the safety and well-being of my son or daughter?

- Do I believe others will care and contribute to my son or daughter's life?

- Am I prepared to take some risks and ask others to help?

- Am I willing to plan now in preparation for the future?

- Am I prepared to share my plan with others?

- guardians if our children are under 19
- friendly support from a trusted source
- links to others in the community
- connections to community resources
- a safety net
- continuity for the family's hopes and wishes

The art of making friends

Did you know that over 50 per cent of the first attempt little kids make to join in a group with other children are rejected?

In other words, the first step in meeting another person is a learned skill that comes with practice. This is a skill that most of us take for granted and which we had to start developing at a very early age. A psychologist, Dr. Michael Guralnick, has observed that children with disabilities often do not experience this trial and error process.

He has suggested that there are three skills which very young children develop while playing with each other:

1. Learning how to initiate contact with our peers.
2. Maintaining play. These are the skills we learn to keep the interaction or relationship going.
3. Conflict resolution. Inevitably in any relationship we have to learn to negotiate, to share, and to compromise.

Friendships rarely develop by chance. We cultivate them as carefully as we nurture a job or a family, a talent or a hobby. Some of us may think that friendships happen naturally and that if they don't occur there is nothing we can do about it. However, there appears to be a certain discipline associated with initiating and developing our acquaintances and friendships.

This discipline may never have begun for people with disabilities. They may have had limited opportunities to be with other people their own age. They may have lived most of their life in a segregated environment. They may have been overprotected. They may have tried to make friends, been unsuccessful, as we all have, and have either given up or not been encouraged to try again. Most importantly, there may never have been the expectation that anyone would care to be their friend or that they would be able to contribute anything to a friendship.

For a variety of reasons, it is often necessary to approach the development of relationships for people with disability in a careful and systematic manner. They do not occur as naturally as they do for others.

How relationships challenge families

While many families recognize the importance of relationships in their loved one's life, they often feel some ambivalence when it comes to actively seeking opportunities for relationships to form. From our experience, there are three challenges that families face in creating relationships: asking, opening, and believing.

ASKING To ask is to make ourselves vulnerable. There is always the possibility of refusal. Yet reaching out and asking is integral to developing and deepening our relationships. Friendships often form because we ask others to participate in a shared activity. We invite acquaintances over for tea to get to know them better. We ask neighbours to help us with building a fence. We ask friends to give us a hand with setting up for a party. Each of these casual invitations presents an opportunity for the relationship to grow.

This process is not so easy when it comes to reaching out on behalf of our sons and daughters. We may feel that extending even casual invitations is risky. We worry that others will feel obliged, or worse, that they might be saying yes because they feel sorry for us or our loved one. This worry speaks to how deeply many of us have been hurt by our culture's devaluing of difference. It makes us forget what our sons and daughters have to offer. It makes us forget that others may care.

We need to remind ourselves of the contributions and richness our sons and daughters have added to our lives and the lives of those around them. There are many, many stories from ordinary people attesting to how their relationship with an isolated or labelled person has changed their life. They are

> The only disability is having no relationship.
> JUDITH SNOW

often people who wanted to reach out but did not know how. Each invitation we offer is an opportunity for others to extend their community and broaden their relationships.

OPENING In order for others to come into our lives there needs to be a place for them. It is impossible to meet people or deepen a friendship if we have no time to spend with others. This is an issue for many people with disabilities. Virtually all areas of their lives may be programmed. To an outsider there is no apparent need for a friend. Friends and acquaintances may find it just too difficult to arrange any time together with your son or daughter. As parents, we may need to give up a program or change schedules to create a space for others to come in.

On a more subtle level, some of our own actions as parents might inhibit the involvement of others. Over the years we may have become used to doing many things for our son or daughter. The presence of others changes our routines. Thinking about another person taking our son or daughter somewhere new might upset us. As we feel ourselves losing some control, we may resist the efforts of others to contribute. We may respond by saying we can do it ourselves. We need to ask ourselves honestly and courageously what we are willing to let go of to make room for others to become active and involved in our children's lives.

When you really think about it, this letting go is our lifetime task as parents. It is why you are reading this book. It is in the best interests of our sons and daughters to be able to manage without us. Friendships provide a catalyst for both of us to accomplish this task. Our sons and daughters grow richer from having experiences outside of the family.

We all separated from our families through friendships. It was our friends who encouraged us to ride our bikes in the streets, ask for a later curfew, and wear different clothing. Each of these events were milestones as we grew into our own. Our loved ones need friends to inspire them to take their own paths as they, too, grow into their own.

BELIEVING Of the three challenges, this may be the great-

Three challenges to families

- Asking
- Opening
- Believing

est. We remember there were no birthday parties or sleepover invitations. We notice yet again someone staring in the supermarket or we receive a pitying look from a passerby. We feel hurt by these things and we ache for our son or daughter. Our overwhelming desire is to protect, and we cannot find it in ourselves to truly believe there is a caring community of people available to befriend our loved one. This lack of belief affects our ability to be open to others, and to trust in their integrity.

Challenging this fear is the growing understanding of our need to be responsible and care for one another in our communities. Rather than being sent off for professional care, people all around us are being supported to live and die in their communities. In spite of the negative view of an uncaring society sold to us every day by the media, people are reaching out to each other more and more. Self-help and support groups thrive in each community. Friends and neighbours are joining together to support a loved one to die at home. Whole neighbourhoods form block watches to look out for one another.

This trend was very much PLAN's experience as well, as we created caring, non-paid, committed relationships for our relatives with disabilities. Church groups and service organizations consistently find people who are prepared and eager to become a part of our loved ones' lives.

Our challenge as parents and as families has been to systematically approach the development of relationships while at the same time addressing our personal fears and biases.

> One's life has value as long as one attributes value to the life of others, by means of love, friendship, and compassion.
> SIMONE DE BEAUVOIR

That's what friends are for

There is something about being human that makes us yearn for the company of others, to be with and to be touched by our family and friends. Isolation and solitude are devastating byproducts of having a disability. This solitude can be even more oppressive in a large impersonal service delivery system. The only way to truly diminish this loneliness is by making deep connections with others. Even though this may be challenging for our sons and daughters, it is critical for

The Inspiration

The Old Testament recounts a story of how the Israelites, led by Joshua, marched around the city of Jericho until by divine miracle, the walls fell down.

In 1980 a small group of people in Ontario, led by Marsha Forest and Judith Snow dedicated themselves to breaking down any walls that prevented Judith from leading a full and active life in her community. They became known as the Joshua Committee.

At the time Judith was living in a Toronto institution, confined to a wheelchair and dependent on attendants to meet all her physical care needs. Her situation was desperate and life-threatening. This group of caring friends and advocates dealt with bureaucrats, politicians, professionals and service providers. Meeting regularly, they overcame any obstacles in Judith's path, from housing, employment, recreation and medical care, to marriage. Still going strong today, this group continues to support Judith.

The Joshua Committee is the inspiration for similar groups around the world. Variously called Circle of Friends, Support Circles, or Personal Networks, they are all dedicated to the same aim — supporting people with disabilities to live a safe, active, and enriched life in the community.

their future security and well-being.

The keys to creating these connections are first, our willingness to let them happen and second, the effort we are prepared to put into making them happen. All the riches of the world will not compensate for the security of being cared for. That's what parents do. That's what friends are for. ■

A circle of friends

Peggie attended school for the first time at the age of nineteen. She was brought to PLAN's attention by a local high-school teacher who was concerned that Peggie was living in the extended care ward of a local hospital. Peggie shared her room with three other women who were in their late seventies. Peggie cannot speak, and they did not appreciate the high-pitched sounds she made.

Peggie had lived in the hospital since the age of two. She had received a severe head injury as a result of a car accident and was immobile. Her family, unable to care for her, had eventually stopped visiting. Peggie had no other companions. Her only stimulation was a TV that she could not see. Most of the time she lay on her back, unable to move or to communicate.

She was isolated, lonely and bored.

PLAN agreed to create a circle of friends for Peggie. At the time we were a new organization and had limited funds. Nevertheless our board of directors were moved by Peggie's story and committed to improving the quality of her life.

We hired a facilitator to get to know Peggie and then to recruit people willing to spend time with her. Finding four people interested in Peggie and willing to visit with her wasn't a problem. However, the hospital was. They soon became defensive, and were threatened by the questions about Peggie's care raised by her new friends.

Matters came to a head. PLAN got word the hospital had recommended that all of Peggie's teeth should be removed. The hospital felt this would be more convenient for staff who fed her. It took Peggie longer to chew her food and staff decided it would be easier to feed her pureed food if she had no teeth. Fortunately PLAN's president and executive director are respected advocates. They were able to use their influence with the Ministry of Health to reverse the decision.

PLAN was also able to convince senior hospital officials to examine other living options for Peggie. With the active presence of friends and visitors, Peggie's life began to brighten. Contact was made with her family. Government agreed to consider Peggie for placement in a group home they were developing. The local school board agreed to extend Peggie's education for one year past the eligible age. Her eyes began to sparkle. She put on weight.

Today Peggie is a completely different person. Our favourite picture shows Peggie dressed in a beautiful black dress with sheer black stockings outside a downtown Vancouver restaurant just prior to attending a Celine Dion concert! A far cry from the ward of an extended care hospital.

Peggie eventually moved to the group home. And while it is some distance from the hospital, she has maintained contacts with the original members of her circle of friends. At the same time, new friends are entering her life.

My brother and friend

Participating in Bob's Personal Network led his brother to write the following.

For over a year now my friend and brother Bob has been associated with PLAN through his Personal Network. I've watched Bob grow dramatically in confidence, in interpersonal relations, and in verbal skills. Bob's world has expanded due to the network that now surrounds him.

Jean, Bob's network facilitator, has been effective in bringing his network together. Bob is now friends with Jean's husband, Mike. Bob and Mike have enjoyed, among other things, skating, bus-riding, and simply "hanging out." This friendship with Mike has been very important to Bob. Although he has five loving brothers, including myself, I feel we have not always helped Bob become an adult. Bob is no longer "Bobby" although my brothers and I may have been slow to understand this fact.

Bob's relationship with Mike has given him a new, adult standard by which to measure his other relations. He now desires, he almost demands, that relationships with him be on an adult level. I say, "Way to go, Bob!"

Another member of Bob's network who has been very important is Wendy. She has helped him learn valuable skills in a one-on-one relation with a peer of the opposite sex, which is something that has been noticeably lacking in Bob's life in the past.

I have learned as much about myself during the past six months as I have about Bob. His growth has challenged me to grow as well and together we are now involved in regular activities such as bowling and soccer. We share a new and dynamic friendship which encourages us both to meet each other's needs and to meet the needs of the important others in our lives.

Letters from Michael

When Michael's mother died, his Personal Network became his sole source of support. Michael is a keen letter writer to PLAN. Here are excerpts from two of his letters.

LETTER ONE

Dear PLAN:

Since I started with my Personal Network, it has been an interesting and very positive experience for me because it is helping me prepare for my future. I am thankful to have wonderful friends come to my first meeting, although I was somewhat disappointed that some couldn't make it to the meeting as they had others things to do.

I have admiration and respect for my network facilitator, Ken. He knows what he is doing and is a great friend; he understands people who have disabilities. By working together with my facilitator and people in my network, along with my mother, as long as she is around, I will be guaranteed a positive and hopeful future.

LETTER TWO, TWO YEARS LATER

Dear Ken and members of PLAN:

The birthday party at the Unitarian Church on July 13th was excellent. I'm pleased a good number showed up, but with regret plenty of people invited couldn't make it because summer is a time people are away on vacation.

The food was wonderful and I liked the cake for the occasion. It's great to have a party like this one to show that there are people who are caring, loving and supportive. I was so happy to get plenty of cards.

This is my first birthday of being on my own. This year I won't have to worry about my mother and no more stressful situations of being concerned whether she'll get better or worse now that the Lord has taken my mother home to that wonderful and happy place where there's no more illness, no more pain, no more suffering. She won't have to go to hospital again.

On the day of my 50th birthday, July 17th, I had lunch at the Sirloiner, and some of the people from my network showed up. This helped make my day a very pleasant one.

My friend Rick

By Debbie, a member of Rick's Personal Network

I first met Rick four years ago when I was working for PLAN. At the time I needed someone to help me get the newsletters folded, stuffed and mailed. Rick volunteered. I liked Rick immediately and soon after, when I was asked if I would join his network, I didn't hesitate to say, "yes."

I'll never forget the first network meeting that we held. Rick's circle of friends really only consisted of his immediate family, and I thought to myself how limited his social and emotional support network was. Rick was very shy. It was difficult for him to participate in our discussions and he often let us make decisions for him. The Rick I know today is quite different!

Over the years the network has grown and there is now a mix of family, neighbours, and friends like myself. We have helped Rick find job opportunities; we've facilitated social activities; and we've just "been there" when he's needed to talk. The most important thing, though, is that he's become part of our lives.

Rick has been part of my family since before my son was three and before my daughter was born. He often comes to stay for dinner or overnight. Sometimes he invites my husband, who works near his apartment, over for lunch.

Recently Rick moved to his own apartment. The network pitched in to make it happen for him and we are in regular contact with him to see how things are going. Rick is a changed man from when I first met him. Being self-sufficient has given him a new confidence and he is much more outgoing. In fact, he often turns down my invitations because he's too busy!

It's been a great four years and I'd like to thank Rick for being my friend. It's not often I get to make friends with a truly kind and sincere person like him.

Worksheet 4

THE WEB OF FRIENDSHIP

The sample web has already been filled out. To fill out your own web:

1. Write your loved one's name in the centre circle.

2. The inner circle represents the area in your loved one's life that is filled with people s/he trusts, feels comfortable with, and confides in. They can be friends or family. However, exclude anyone in a paid position. The people in this circle will have a reciprocal relationship with your relative, based on friendship and respect.

3. The remainder of the web represents the rest of the people who are involved in your loved one's life. Write their names down, using the distance from the centre to represent how close their relationship is.

4. If you wish, the dotted lines can be used to indicate the different areas in your loved one's life. For example, family in the top section, friends on the left, school and work in the other quadrants. This will help you to visually demonstrate the interrelationships in your loved one's life.

5. When you have completed this picture, think about how you can strengthen the web, by joining up the people in your loved one's life. In a different coloured pen, draw in all the potential connections.

Sample web

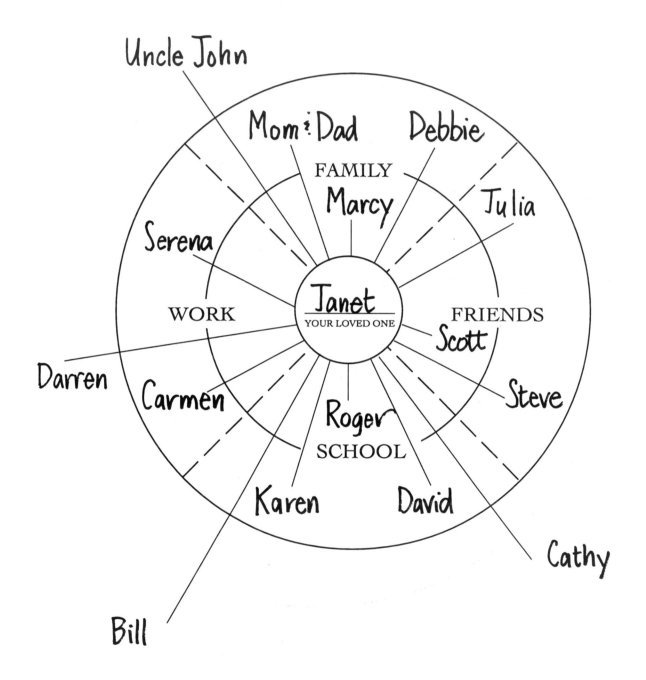

Your loved one's web

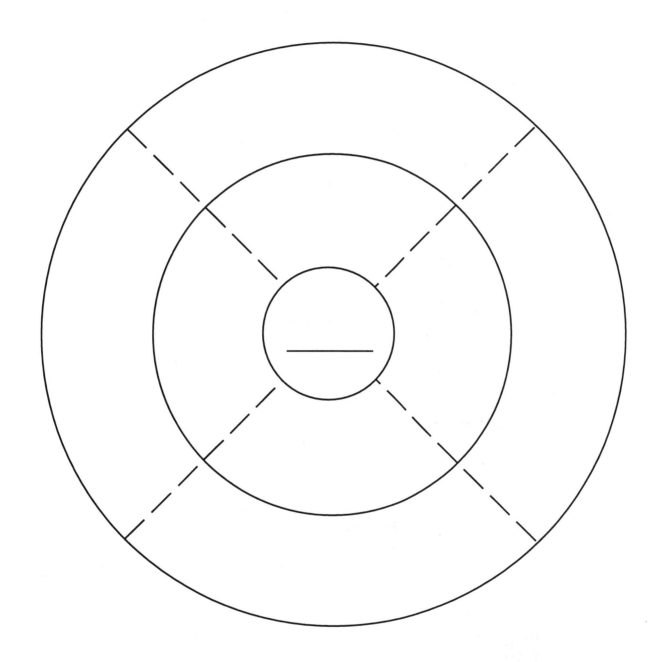

Controlling the Home Environment

Home is where
the Heart is.
PLINY THE ELDER

Home alone too!

"MY WIFE AND I had always expected that Rick would stay in our home. We thought perhaps the local association would take it over after we died, and turn it into a group home. Then Rick and others like him would live there.

"After attending a workshop on 'Letting Go,' I began to wonder whether I was holding onto ideas that weren't in Rick's best interest. I had no idea if he would enjoy living with other people. I didn't know how he'd react to having staff supervising him. Well, actually I did know. Rick had lived in a group home years before and it hadn't worked out.

"Maybe I'm being a little stubborn here, I thought. Maybe it would not be best for Rick after all.

"I thought I'd better take this up with Rick. He didn't think too much of the idea at first. Then all of a sudden it was decided, Rick would move. Rick and his circle decided that is, not me. It was quite a shock."

Their neighbour across the street who had been invited to the first meeting knew of a vacancy in an apartment building that was centrally located. So Rick moved out last February. "It's a start," says George. "The apartment's his home now – he doesn't have his old man to bug him there.

"Fortunately there have been no big problems. He took it in his stride. Actually he has matured quite a bit as a result of the move. He likes to boast that he knows all 15 people in the building and they all talk to him. What a difference from his old neighborhood where so many of the people he knew had moved away. And I must admit I like the idea he is surrounded by people who accept him and in their own way check up on him."

And there's more. Rick has just found a two-bedroom apartment in the same building. Bob, his friend since childhood, is moving in with him. George suspects Rick has at least one more move ahead of him and that it will be into a place he owns himself. ■

Controlling the Home Environment

A home of one's own. This is a significant dream for most of us. A home, particularly one we own, represents stability and security. It also ensures privacy, and gives us an opportunity to shape our living space according to our wishes and creativity. Home ownership is a good investment, and a hedge against inflationary times.

The value of a home of one's own is universal. It is recognized as a place of hospitality and as a haven by people everywhere. It is no coincidence that the logo of the International Year of the Family in 1994 was a heart-shaped roof. Home is compatible with family. The word, home, comes from a Sanskrit root meaning a safe place to lie down; a separation of outside from inside, defined by a threshold.

Most of us view home ownership as a given. This is not so for people with disabilities. For most it is not even a consideration, not even in their vocabulary. It is a dream they dare not consider. The same may be true for their parents. The closest many of us get to the dream is a secret desire to leave our home to an agency that will guarantee to care for our children as long as they live. Other than that, ownership is simply out of the picture. Or so we think. That secret desire is a critical strand, however. As we pull it, it will lead to other possibilities: stability, permanence, predictability, order, control and choice.

> In building the future for your son or daughter, are you the architect?
> ARTHUR MUDRY

Choice is the issue

Homeowners have status in our society. The pride of ownership is one of our more important cultural values. Home ownership is the fulfilment of a dream even if we have a hefty mortgage and are renting money from a financial institution.

Home ownership means ...

- Control over where you live

- Stability of tenure

- The opportunity to build up equity

- Investment

- A hedge against inflation

- Privacy

- A sense of place

- Choice

- Contemplation

- Ability to offer hospitality

- A haven

- Security

- Safety, comfort

Owning your own place or at least having control over your living environment is about choice, control and status. We see no reason why people who need staff support for their personal care should be denied the benefits of a home of their own. There are many stories revealing the dramatic changes in the lives of people when they control their home environment. That is why we believe controlling the home environment is such an important step in the Personal Future Plan you are developing.

Many of us cannot afford to assist our sons and daughters to purchase their own home. We're still paying down our own mortgage! There are alternatives to home ownership however, that still provide choice, control and status. Housing equity cooperatives, land trusts and co-housing have many of the advantages of home ownership. If these options are not available or appropriate, we suggest you consider rental. Rental accommodation, particularly long-term based, can allow people to establish a sense of their own place and to maintain control of their living environment. Being a tenant provides a much different status than being a resident of a group home.

So even if you cannot afford to buy a house at the present time, we suggest you reflect on the issues raised in this chapter. "Controlling" our loved ones' home environment is one way we can increase the amount of influence and direction they will have over their lives.

This third step will not work in isolation from the other steps. Without the existence of a network of personal support, our sons and daughters will be just as isolated in their own place as anywhere else. Similarly, you will need to use your will and trust agreement to formalize the arrangements to own or rent as well as to maintain your loved one's housing. Step 4, Preparing for Decision-Making, will provide you with some options to protect your relative against exploitation and to monitor the quality of life. In this way the various steps of the Personal Future Plan you are preparing are interrelated.

Home base: a lesson learned

We've got an admission to make. If this book had been written two years ago, there would not have been a section on home ownership or on the importance of loved ones' controlling the home environment they live in. We saw housing as just another service that needed to be secured and monitored. We failed to appreciate just how fundamental to our daily lives is the place we live in. More than that, we actually resisted any requests to provide more information on home ownership. We did not see the relevance to the future planning model we had in mind.

Well, we goofed!

In virtually every contact with families, the topic of home ownership surfaced. Most families wanted to know if it were possible to leave the family home to a non-profit society in exchange for lifelong tenure for their loved one with a disability. Some were actually interested in purchasing a house outright. It became clear that the hopes and dreams of many families are associated with the place their loved one lives in. It finally sunk in – the home is the base upon which the other plans of future security can be built.

This experience led PLAN to reconsider the essential components of creating a secure future for people with disabilities. A place to live, a place where one could direct the rest of one's life, was integral to the other components of a Personal Future Plan. And so we took the lead and in association with five other organizations created the Home Ownership Means Equity (HOME) Advisory Service for families (see page 66).

Thanks to the parents we met in our travels, we now see the importance of disentangling or separating the house or home from the other support services our children receive. And we now see the importance of having "a place of one's own." How could we have missed it!

Making homes out of houses

Here are some questions that will get you and your family thinking about establishing a household for your loved one:
- What kind of housing is s/he interested in?
- What kind of support staff will s/he need?
- Who among friends and acquaintances would make compatible roommates?

- What kind of home can you imagine your loved one living in?
- Where would the best location for the home be?
- Which other families could you enter into a joint purchase with?
- Who would be interested in supporting your loved one to establish a household?

Limitations of current housing options

Despite the millions of dollars governments spend on the cost of accommodation and shelter for people with disabilities, none of it assists them to control their home. As a result, more and more families are looking for alternatives. That is not to say that group homes or semi-independent living or some of the other residential options are wrong. But they have their limitations.

Regardless of whether your son or daughter is currently living with you or in a residential service provided by someone else, you have likely experienced some or all of these frustrations:

- Limited new housing spaces become available each year.
- Waiting lists are long.
- Housing is not available close to where you live or in familiar neighbourhoods.
- Group homes often become places of work for staff rather than homes for the people who actually live there.
- Staff turnover can be high.
- Someone else decides who your loved one lives with.
- Individual needs may be secondary to those of other roommates.
- Number of unrelated people living together is higher than typical.
- Rules, procedures, and protocols abound.
- The personality of the home is shaped by the people who work there, not by the people who live there.
- There is anxiety about family involvement.
- Licensing restricts the character and look of the house.

Home control means …

- Choosing where you want to live.

- Choosing whom you will live with.

- Choosing the staff who will support you.

- Agency priorities and politics influence what happens in the house as much as the needs and interests of the people who live there.

Control is the key

The alternative is to put control in the hands of our loved ones, or at least in the hands of their representatives. Control is best exercised by ownership. The alternative is for our sons and daughters to own their home themselves. They can own it directly or it can be owned on their behalf through a trust.

This has become an increasingly attractive option to parents who want a secure housing option to complement the other elements of the Personal Future Plan they are developing. They see their sons or daughters living in a place they choose, with people they choose, with staff they choose to hire (or fire), for as long as they like. Actually that sounds sterile. They see their child or relative residing in a good friendly neighbourhood, within walking distance of stores and other amenities, greeted by neighbours and shopkeepers, living with a best friend, hosting dinner parties, and relaxing in a home designed and decorated to his or her tastes. Too good to be true? Read the article, "Lynn Has a Home of Her Own," on page 71, and consider the housing examples at the end of this chapter.

Critical components of home ownership

Taking matters into your own hands requires more work. It means paying attention to a number of critical components, including:

FINANCING THE PURCHASE
Unless you are independently wealthy, this is the most formidable and intimidating challenge. At the present time there are no tax concessions or favourable tax treatment for families who want to pursue home ownership for their children with disabilities. We see this as one of the critical lobby issues which families need to pursue with their provincial and

JOINT TENANCY
Property owned jointly by two or more persons in which the surviving joint tenant(s) becomes the owner of the entire property when one of the joint tenants dies.

TENANCY IN COMMON
Property owned jointly by two or more people. Upon the death of one of the tenants-in-common, ownership of the deceased's shares is transferred to that person's estate, not to the other joint owner.

federal governments. How about a Registered Home Ownership Savings Plan for People with Disabilities, for example?

In the meantime families have opted to:
- Re-mortgage the family home.
- Form a partnership with other parents to purchase a home.
- Take out a reverse mortgage.
- Join with developers who will reduce the price in return for zoning concessions from municipalities.
- Earmark part of their estate to establish a housing trust exclusively for the purpose of purchasing a home.
- Purchase life insurance to finance a home or establish a housing trust.
- Rent out the other bedrooms to help finance mortgage payments.

OWNERSHIP
Here are some home ownership options you may want to consider for your loved one:
- S/he has direct title.
- S/he co-owns the house with another person.
- You own the house together.
- At least two families own the home.
- S/he lives in a co-op that can build up equity.
- You arrange financing for your loved one to live in a co-housing development. All financing (for each unit and the common areas) comes from the owners of all the units.
- The house is owned by a trust in your child or relative's name (or by joint trusts if two or more people with disabilities are involved). The trust(s) can be established:
  – while you are alive, or
  – through your estate after your death.

Types of co-ownership
If more than one individual or family own the home, you must choose one of these legal co-ownership options:
- joint tenancy; or
- tenancy in common.

HOUSING TYPES
Just about anything is possible:

- single family
- condominium or row housing
- housing cooperative unit
- co-housing
- apartment
- mobile home
- infill housing (e.g., converting a garage into a small housing unit)
- renovation of existing house
- purpose-built housing designed for your loved one's needs. Example: shared kitchen, dining and lounge areas.

ONGOING MAINTENANCE

If you purchase a house, you will need to make arrangements to cover:

The ongoing mortgage payments.
- Will government income assistance be enough?
- When you are alive, will the difference come out of a trust or from some other source?
- After your death, will the difference come out of a trust?

The major maintenance, repair and insurance costs as well as property taxes.
- Will you pay for these yourself while you are alive? Or will you establish a living trust for this purpose?
- Will you establish a trust to cover these costs after your death?

    NOTE It is critical that you consult with a knowledgeable lawyer to establish the trusts referred to above. For example, you may want to ensure that you do not jeopardize your loved one's entitlement to government benefits.

The minor, ongoing maintenance.
While this can be done by yourself in the short term, you may want to consider contracting with a property management company to provide this service. In addition, this may be a service you will need to request your trustee to provide. Obviously, if your loved one lives in a condominium or cooperative, property maintenance is already built into the housing agreement.

Mid pleasures and places though we may roam, Be it ever so humble, there's no place like home.
JOHN HOWARD PAYNE

NEGOTIATING FUNDING FOR PROGRAM SUPPORT STAFF

Unless you have the private means to pay for staffing supports, you will have to negotiate funding from government. Generally government is becoming more interested in supporting people to live in their own homes. After all, it represents a big savings to them if the capital costs of the home are not their responsibility. We suggest you use this argument when negotiating the supports necessary. You can argue that you, the family, finance the house; they, the government, finance staff supports.

SELECTING COMPATIBLE SUPPORT STAFF

Not every staff person will be comfortable working in your loved one's private home. Many will see it primarily as their workplace. We suggest you spend time clarifying in writing the values that are important to your child or relative. Whether hiring from an agency or society, become familiar with their operating philosophy. Interview their executive director. Visit some of their programs. Get to meet the people who receive services from them; talk to their families.

Home Ownership Means Equity (HOME)

In response to a growing interest in pursuing the home ownership alternatives, a group of families from the Lower Mainland of British Columbia have created a support service. The HOME Advisory Service provides families with hands-on advice and support to deal with the potentially complex issues involved with home purchase.

The HOME Advisory Service will:
- link families with others who may be interested in sharing purchase costs
- liaise with builders, developers and financial institutions
- assist with negotiating a service contract or program supports with government
- provide sample clauses
- refer to knowledgeable professionals
- assist with finding a friendly, compatible roommate
- provide advice and consultation on all the critical components of home ownership

For information about HOME, call the PLAN office: 439-9566

Do not be afraid to let staff go if it appears they are not compatible with the values established for the home.

CHOOSING A COMPATIBLE ROOMMATE

There is no scientific approach to this challenge. Some people are easy to get along with. Others aren't. Often you won't know until you try. Many of the people we know who are now living in their own homes first tried living "on their own" in some form of rental accommodation. Then they invited someone to live with them. This is an excellent way to test the kinds of support you will need. It also enables people to have a better sense of who they want in a roommate.

TECHNICAL ADVICE FOR CONSTRUCTION AND RENOVATION

We'll leave you to your own devices with this component. You will be able to access building contractors in your area far better than we will. Certainly accessible building design advice would be available from local disability resource groups if you would like additional expertise. Other parents are a good connection for families who are considering construction or renovation. Also don't forget to contact the HOME Advisory Service at PLAN. (See page 66.)

Looking to the future

Times are changing. More people with disabilities are about to become home owners. They are gaining a measure of choice and control over their lives they have never experienced before. When established with due respect and consideration for the issues identified here, home ownership also provides parents with a concrete component of their Personal Future Plan.

As government financial support for social housing declines or is eliminated, families will have to examine other sources of financing. Families see themselves as part of the solution. With tax and trust concessions, more and more families will be willing and able to invest in the housing future of their children and to support those whose families are unable to. ■

Examples of housing solutions

Given the complexity of issues and the unique circumstances of each individual and family, the following examples should serve only as illustrations of what is possible.

EXAMPLE ONE
Patricia, living in an apartment.

Background

Patricia is a 38-year-old woman who lives on her own. She receives the maximum Income Assistance benefits available from the Ministry of Social Services. After sharing a rental apartment with a friend for three years, Patricia moved into a housing cooperative where she stayed for two years.

Patricia's grandmother had left her a large sum of money which she had placed in a discretionary trust. John, Patricia's father, is trustee.

When Patricia decided to move out of the housing co-op, she and her dad decided to look for an apartment unit she could own. They found an affordable one-bedroom unit, centrally located near a large shopping centre, close to major bus routes and a short walk to the Skytrain.

Financing

The apartment unit cost $125,000.

Patricia's dad contributed $ 12,500 of his own money.

The discretionary trust contributed $97,500 in a no-interest second mortgage.

Patricia took out a first mortgage for $15,000.

Features
- Patricia has title to the apartment.
- Since her dad owns only a tenth of the apartment, Patricia is the principal owner. As homeowner she is eligible for the homeowner's grant. Also since this is her principal residence, the apartment is not subject to capital gains should it ever be sold.
- The fact that Patricia's father owns approximately a tenth of the apartment prevents a dishonest person from persuading Patricia to sell or to order major repairs.
- Should the apartment ever be sold, Patricia's father would get his money back and the amount of the second mortgage would be returned to the discretionary trust.
- The mortgage payments plus hydro and maintenance costs are equal to the shelter component of the Income Assistance Patricia receives.

EXAMPLE TWO
Thomas, staying in the family home.

Background
Thomas is a 48-year-old man who currently lives with his parents. His parents want him to remain in the family home after they die. When that day arrives, the house will be placed in a trust for Thomas's continued use. To support

Thomas, the family has arranged to establish two trusts (a residential trust and a family trust – described below) and a micro board (described on page 87). They have also arranged to recruit a "support family."

Financing

The parents' estate plan provides for the home, including furnishings, to be left in a discretionary trust for the primary use and benefit of Thomas. The family calls this the "residential trust." The trust would have a small amount of funds to cover minor repairs.

A separate discretionary financial trust will provide additional assets to cover maintenance of the home, property taxes, extraordinary expenses, and the quality of Thomas's life. The family calls this the "family trust."

The Ministry of Social Services will be asked to contribute funding towards the daily support needs of Thomas – his daily food, shelter, and personal support.

Features

- Thomas continues to live in an environment that is most familiar to him.
- The financing provided by government for Thomas's support needs will be less than that required for a conventional group home.
- None of the money from government will be applied to the capital cost or maintenance of the home.
- There will be a small "micro board"(see page 87 for details about micro boards).This micro board consists of three people (a family member/advo-

cate, a co-trustee, and a Personal Network member). This micro board will have the authority to contract with the Ministry of Social Services for funding on Thomas's behalf. This funding will allow them to contract with service providers. They will also monitor the quality of the care.

- A support family of two or more compatible people will live in the home with Thomas and provide a caring and harmonious living environment. In return, they will live rent free and enjoy the home as is customary under traditional rental contracts.
- Should it become necessary to sell the home, the will contains a provision that the trustees can do so and use the funds from this transaction to acquire an equivalent home for Thomas's benefit. Any surplus funds will be placed in the "family trust."

EXAMPLE THREE
Jennifer, living in a co-housing development.

Background

Mr. and Mrs. Howe have purchased a three-bedroom townhouse unit in the Windsong Co-Housing development in Langley, for their daughter Jennifer.

Co-housing is a term applied to housing projects where the owners pay the costs for their own unit as well as their portion of the common area. Co-housing attracts people who want to recreate a "village atmosphere." It is a modern way of building a support network or creating a supportive community, and this is what interested the Howes. People share meals together and are committed to building a safe, caring place for everyone.

The Howes have worked out an arrangement to obtain an affordable unit for their daughter and at the same time maintain a modest retirement income for themselves.

Financing

Cost of the three bedroom unit including design modifications for Jennifer's wheelchair is $200,000.

Mr. and Mrs. Howe purchased the unit outright and gave Jennifer a demand mortgage.

The approximately $1200 a month mortgage will be recovered from three sources:

- Jennifer's GAIN benefits;
- renting out one of the bedrooms to a third party who will provide some support to Jennifer; and
- Social Services, who are currently funding Jennifer's shelter costs at a group home she lives in.

Features

- The parents, who are retired, derive all their income from investments. They sunk their investments into the unit for Jennifer but they will derive a monthly income from the mortgage payments.
- Jennifer enjoys the benefits of living in a supportive community she has been a member of from the beginning.
- Windsong incorporates a glass-covered pedestrian street. Each of the 34 units opens onto an unheated glassed-in atrium as well. These design features

are perfect for Jennifer.

- Jennifer has title to her unit and therefore is eligible for the homeowner's grant.

EXAMPLE FOUR

Surrinder, living in a condominium near the family home.

Background

Mr. and Mrs. Singh purchased a two-bedroom condominium for their 28-year-old son, Surrinder. The complex is located within three blocks of the family home.

Financing

Total cost of condominium: $170,000.

Down payment from the parents: $140,000.

Surrinder's monthly mortgage payments are approximately $300 over a twenty year period.

Features

- Ownership of the home is between the parents and Surrinder. As financial protection, the parents have enduring power of attorney.
- Upon the parents' death, complete ownership of the home goes to Surrinder. Surrinder's sister and her husband will have power of attorney.
- One of the bedrooms will be rented to a roommate for Surrinder.
- A committee comprised of a representative of the family, the service delivery organization, and the family of Surrinder's roommate will oversee the maintenance and operation of the condominium.

Lynn has a home of her own

Like many senior couples who have worked hard all their lives, Arthur and Hazel own their own home. Also like many couples, they felt they had accumulated sufficient assets to leave a trust fund for their daughter, Lynn, after they died. Unlike many couples, however, Arthur and Hazel have found a way to creatively use their assets for Lynn's benefit today.

In response to a crisis in Lynn's life that left her without an appropriately secure place to live, Arthur and Hazel purchased a house for their daughter. "We had always intended to leave our assets to be divided among our three children after we die. We simply shifted that inevitable line forward 20 or 30 years to secure what Lynn needs right now."

Until the age of 28, Lynn had enjoyed a happy fulfilled life in the family home. Then Lynn moved into a group home. Lynn became increasingly depressed to the point of being unwilling to leave the house. "It was as if she descended deep into a cave," recalls her father. "The chaos to her psyche in that particular situation was devastating to Lynn. She had lost contact with the world."

Lynn spent two subsequent years at Birch Clinic before her family were willing to look for a place in the community again. However, the options all looked the same. "Group homes seemed little more than mini-institutions. Agency homes did not feel like the homes the rest of us live in," Arthur said.

That's when they decided to buy Lynn her own home. They had two criteria. First, her home should be within walking distance of the family home. Secondly, it should be near to the shops, recreation centre and library. It seemed like an impossible dream.

But dreams do shape reality, and with persistence and good fortune they were able to find an old small house within two blocks of the family home. After months of exhaustive renovations, Lynn had her own place to her satisfaction. This special moment was enhanced because Lynn could share it with her new housemate, her old schoolmate and long-time family friend, Sarah Barker.

Arthur and Hazel remortgaged the family home. As Arthur describes it, "We've been paying rent to the mortgage on our own house for most of our life. We're just continuing this practice in order that Lynn may have her own house. The mortgage collateral is on the family home so if anything happens to us, Lynn's house is secure."

Next, Arthur and Hazel had to find compatible care-givers. This proved to be a difficult task. Lynn and Sarah needed support in the evening between 3:30 and 10:00 p.m. Primarily, this was to be Sarah and Lynn's home, not a place of work for staff. Eventually they settled on an agency, largely because the executive director expressed his commitment to keeping the emphasis on Lynn and Sarah, and "their" home.

The next step was to create a support network of caring family and friends who are committed to maintaining Lynn's quality of life. To that end, Arthur and Hazel have a micro board and are involved in developing a Personal Network for Lynn.

Preparing for Decision-Making

Every blade of
grass has its angel
that bends over it
and whispers,
"Grow, grow."

THE TALMUD

More than we bargained for

"THERE WAS A PERIOD when Rick didn't live with us, you know. At the time we thought we were doing the right thing. He was getting pretty big and we thought he'd be better off with people his own age. My wife and I were both working, and we thought it would be best for all of us."

George's voice softens as he discusses what he calls Rick's little adventure. Rick moved to a farm community where he lived in a group home with eight other young people his own age.

"At first it went OK. For Rick, that is. Not for us. We were in shock for weeks. Driving away from that home was the hardest thing I ever had to do next to burying my wife. Anyway, new people, and new things to do everyday kept Rick happy for a while."

Rick is quite transparent. It is easy to tell if he's happy or not. He wouldn't tell George and his wife what was bothering him but after a while he looked so glum they knew something was wrong. It took them some time to get to the bottom of it.

One night George had popped over to the house to drop off some strawberries he had just picked at the U-Pick down the road. Staff were watching television and the residents were all in their rooms. It turned out that this was common practice. In fact, it was the nightly routine. The evening shift was sending everyone to their own room at 8:30 every evening. No one was allowed to watch TV, use a radio or tape deck, or make any noise.

"It was just like the bloody Air Force, back in World War Two," George explains. "No, it was worse. Lights out over there was at 10:00 p.m. for the crews who had to be up early for a flying mission. As long as we observed the blackout we could do what we pretty well wanted to."

Rick's life was completely regulated at the home, George explained.

"Their lives were controlled from top to bottom. Heck, in the six months he was there, he had four supervisors. It was a regular revolving door. Even the little things were controlled. One supervisor lasted five days. His big thing was to serve all the food from pots on the stove. After he was gone the next supervisor changed the "policy." All food was to be placed in serving dishes on the table! That's the way it worked for everything. No privacy, no respect, and no choice."

It was too much for Rick and his parents. George and his wife invited Rick to move back home.

"We thought we were giving Rick more choices when he moved into the group home. Instead, we got more than we bargained for."

One of the things that bothered Rick about his group home experience was the withdrawal of his spending privileges. Any of his own money, including the

continued on page 76

Preparing for Decision-Making

When you get right down to it, what do parents really want for their children? On the one hand we want to protect our children from discrimination, exploitation, abuse, neglect and injury. In other words, we want to keep them safe. On the other hand, we want to assert their essential humanity, and to focus on similarities, not differences. We want to teach them to survive through adversity, as all of us must. We want to champion their autonomy, to enhance their life's experiences, to nurture their abilities, hopes and dreams. We want to declare their worthiness and give them a life worth living.

Unfortunately, we may resign ourselves to keeping them safe, lacking confidence that we can make any other difference in their lives.

Therein lies the challenge. It's a delicate balancing act faced by families the world over: keeping their loved ones safe while at the same time respecting their choices.

Make no mistake about it. This balancing act is a tough challenge. Families find it hard. So does government and its institutions. If it were easy we wouldn't need to devote a chapter to the topic. No one has yet discovered how to create the perfect world for anyone, let alone for people with disabilities.

- Is it better to be safe than sorry?

- Is offering choice too chancy?

- How big a risk are we prepared to take?

- Can we balance safety with choice?

Government's response

As parents, we know there are no absolute guarantees for keeping people with disabilities safe while at the same time respecting their choices. Nevertheless, families have tended to rely on government and its institutions to resolve the dilemma. The three most common tools at government's dis-

"comforts allowance" he received from government, had to be placed in a bank account that could be accessed by staff. And they often did, buying things he didn't ask for or want.

"Rick isn't a whiz with money but he is careful," George explained. "After my wife died I decided that since he was never going to live in a government-funded home, I didn't have to worry about government social assistance for Rick. I had enough money put aside, thanks to my wife's careful investments. On top of that I was able to buy a life insurance policy outright, cash on the barrel. That will increase the size of Rick's estate quite a bit."

George was quite worried that Rick would be taken advantage of by some unscrupulous person. He wanted Rick to have easy access to his money, but he wanted some checks on his spending. So he set up a trust. Not a discretionary trust but an income trust.

"I've got the local credit union acting as my trustee now. They're good at managing and investing the money. But just to make sure they keep Rick's interests in mind, I've appointed a co-trustee from the Personal Network. And to top it all off, my will instructs the trustees to also seek advice from PLAN. All this may sound complicated, but it acts like a system of checks and balances.

"When all is said and done, I'm finally getting what I bargained for. Rick's interests are respected and so are mine. You can't beat that." ■

Worksheet 5 – Joint Decision-Making

This worksheet is based on the three major areas of decision-making: health/medical decisions; financial decisions; and personal decisions. The worksheet is located at the end of this section, on page 94. Have a look at it now, then fill it out when you've finished reviewing this material.

posal are programs and services; regulations and policy; and legal guardianship. Let's look at how well these tools respond to the twin goals of keeping people safe while respecting choices.

PROGRAMS AND SERVICES

A wide range of human services, professional supports, and social, health and educational programs exist to support people with disabilities. There are some drawbacks, however:

- Funding for these programs and services is already limited and is coming under increasing restraint.
- Staff turnover is high.
- Programs and services cannot respond to every area of human need, particularly the need for friendship and companionship.
- Control is invariably in the hands of the service provider, not the individual or friends and families.
- People can be isolated in services, preventing community connections and relationships from developing.

REGULATIONS AND POLICY

As our service delivery system has evolved and become more sophisticated, so have the rules and regulations governing practice and provision of care. Nevertheless, mistreatment, abuse and neglect still occur. We know this from our own experiences as well as from the media's tragic portrayal of those who slip through the system.

In our rush to protect and prevent, we encourage government to create regulations. However, the step-by-step expansion of government regulations eventually develops into a virtual straight-jacket:

- Rules and regulations become more important than human flexibility and common sense.
- Following the rules is encouraged; creativity and initiative aren't.
- Insurance requirements push considerations of risk and liability into the foreground.
- The sheer weight of regulations interferes with real caring.
- Everything important to people is lost in highly regulated environments.
- A culture of mistrust is created in which there must always be someone to blame.
- Union agreements can create additional constraints.
- Bureaucracy is created to monitor the rules, adding another significant expense to the cost of caring.

> Do unto others as you would have them do unto you.
> THE GOLDEN RULE

LEGAL GUARDIANSHIP

Our society has created legal mechanisms to allow another person to take over all the affairs and decision-making of someone who has been judged incapable by court order. That guardian then has complete power to make financial, medical and legal decisions for the person. In B.C., this arrangement is called committeeship.

Again, this system is not perfect. There is a country-wide movement in Canada to reform guardianship legislation. British Columbia, Saskatchewan, Quebec, Ontario and the Yukon are working on changes to laws that were developed forty or fifty years ago.

Here are some of the concerns about legal guardianship:

- Most guardianship orders are "all or nothing." Even though individuals may need help only in certain areas of decision-making, all of their financial and personal decision-making power is removed.
- A full guardianship order strips individuals of all citizenship rights. In the eyes of the law, they are no longer persons.
- Guardianship doesn't recognize that most of us make decisions in collaboration with others, be they friends or family.
- People with intellectual impairments and other noticeable

differences are usually presumed to be incapable.
- Ability to communicate verbally is traditionally associated with capacity.
- Obtaining a guardianship order is costly and time-consuming.

Four false assumptions

Society's quest to develop tools that keep people safe and guarantee the quality of their life is based on four false assumptions:

1. It is possible to create a perfect system.
2. All bad things that happen to people can be prevented with a sufficient body of law and regulation.
3. A paid professional's response is the only response to the situation of a person in need.
4. Safety and protection are valid ends in themselves, rather than a means to enhancing the quality of a person's life.

Joint decision-making

Imagine all the changes that have taken place in our world. Some are earth-shaking; some we barely notice at all. Change is a constant for everyone, including people with disabilities. Nobody really knows what our loved ones will have to adjust to in their lives. We can make some educated guesses, but there are no guarantees.

Rather than spending time trying to predict the future, we suggest that you focus on preparing for good decision-making. Good decision-making ensures the best possible input is available to assist our sons and daughters adjust to change. Good decision-making is joint decision-making.

Despite the need for our sons and daughters to make their own decisions, there is this sad reality: unlike our own decision-making, their decisions are usually made by someone else, often without any consultation.

In practical terms, they are offered few choices in their lives. As parents we can be guilty of this; so can service providers and professionals. Whatever the reasons – and

Joint decision-making for our loved one means:

- They actively participate.
- Their views are sought and taken into consideration.
- They are surrounded by caring, knowledgeable, trustworthy people who can assist with their decision-making, and communicate their decisions.
- Their needs are the primary consideration, not those of staff or the service system.
- The focus is on their abilities.

- All their choices and options are considered.
- Their tastes, preferences, motives and ability to discriminate are taken seriously.
- Their risks, failures and mistakes are learning opportunities.
- Their intuition and feelings are considered, along with intellectual ability.
- All their methods of communication, both verbal and non-verbal, are recognized as valid.

most of us do it with the best of intentions – our loved ones have few choices and little control over their lives. Their decision-making ability is not accepted and is often ignored. This reality is like a bad habit that does not serve our children well now, and certainly will not serve them in the future.

Should I consider legal guardianship? [1]

Some families believe the only way they can have power to protect their adult son or daughter, especially in dealing with the service systems or professionals who seem to control their lives, is to become their legal guardian. As we have discussed above, this is a very intrusive and costly solution. And from a practical point of view, we believe it is unnecessary.

We know our sons and daughters have interests, preferences, and desires. We want to ensure that these are not

---

1. The potential for legal guardianship is relevant only for adults with disabilities. Parents are already natural guardians for children under 19. However, you do need to identify guardians for any child in case you die. See p. 105, What happens if I die without a will?

Choices

We suggest that you approach your loved one's role in decision-making by asking yourself the following questions:

• What choices does s/he have now?

• What experience does s/he have with decision-making?

• With support, could s/he be assisted to make decisions independently?

• What decisions can your loved one make independently?

• What decisions will s/he need help with?

• What decisions will others challenge your loved one on?

• What informal arrangements can be made to assist with decision-making?

• What formal or legal arrangements other than guardianship can be made to assist with decision-making?

ignored. Further, we want to guarantee that our loved ones are given choices and that their input is valid. But we want to make sure they are safe. This is not an easy task, and it is inevitably a matter of trial and error.

However, we believe that you can achieve what you want without resorting to legal guardianship. But before you accept our assurances, let's take a look at the major areas of decision-making in your son or daughter's life. We think we can convince you that you can have your cake and eat it too. That is, you can keep your children safe and maximize their choices without resorting to legal guardianship.

Types of decision-making

There are three broad areas of decision-making that affect your loved one's life:
• Health/Medical Decisions
•. Financial Decisions
• Personal Care Decisions

HEALTH/MEDICAL DECISION-MAKING

You can divide this category into emergency and non-emergency decision-making.

Most families are concerned whether their son or daughter will receive medical treatment in the event of an emergency, especially if the doctors are unable to obtain legal consent. You need not worry. Doctors in British Columbia can and do provide medical treatment on an emergency basis without consent.

For non-emergency health care, the experience is more varied. Many adults with disabilities enjoy a long-standing relationship with their family doctor. They know each other's abilities and communication styles. In these situations, the capacity of the person with the disability to give consent is simply not an issue. The physician is willing to take the time to give individuals the opportunity to express their wishes.

In other families, it has become common practice for the doctor or health care provider to ask next-of-kin to authorize health care treatment for the adult with the disability. Even

A note on committees

A committee (pronounced com-mit-TEE) is someone appointed by the court to make decisions on a person's behalf.

Under current legislation (not the new B.C. adult guardianship legislation) there are three forms of committee:

1. Committee of affairs. This gives a committee authority to make financial and legal decisions for someone who is not mentally capable.

2. Committee of the person. This gives a committee authority to make decisions about health and personal care.

3. Committee of both the person and affairs. This gives a committee authority to make both kinds of decisions.

though next-of-kin has no "legal authority," the medical professional recognizes the long-standing relationship of trust and caring.

In these situations joint decision-making is already working.

However, some health care professionals will provide major health care only if the adult with a disability has a court-appointed committee. In these situations, the adult's ability to consent is challenged and informal status for family members is not recognized. As a result, families have had to apply to the courts to become "committee" in order to give consent to an operation or health care procedure.

The new B.C. guardianship legislation recognizes this dilemma. Under that legislation:

- A temporary substitute decision-maker can be appointed to give substitute consent.
- The temporary substitute decision-maker can only be appointed given certain criteria, and within certain restrictions, and after following a process to ensure there is no abuse of the individual's rights.
- A temporary substitute decision-maker may be the adult's spouse, child, parent, sibling or anyone else related to the adult by birth or adoption.

FINANCIAL DECISIONS

In the past many families considered becoming "committee of the person" or "committee of the estate" in order to protect, manage, and invest the financial assets of their adult relative with a disability.

This procedure has a number of disadvantages:
- obtaining "committee" involves the courts and is time-consuming and expensive;
- reporting on the management and expenditure of money is tedious and costly;
- further rights of the person with a disability are removed; and
- guidelines to protect the assets may be too conservative for productive money management.

For many people with a disability the only disposable

Representation Agreements – Recognizing joint decision-making

There are four separate acts in the new B.C. adult guardianship legislation:
1) The Representation Agreement Act
2) The Health Care Consent and Care Facility Admission Act
3) The Adult Guardianship Act
4) The Public Guardian & Trustee Act

The Representation Agreement Act introduces a brand-new approach for assisting people with decision-making. It creates a new mechanism whereby adults can choose the people they want to help them make decisions should the need arise. The representation agreement will allow people with disabilities to choose one or more people to be their "representatives." Their "representatives" will have authority to assist or make decisions about their health and personal care as well as their legal and financial affairs. Representation agreements will replace enduring powers of attorney.

The basic representation agreement provides an opportunity for everyone, including people with disabilities, to develop a joint decision-making document that gives status to people they are in a caring, trusting relationship with.

Here are some features of the representation agreement which may be applicable to adults with disabilities:
- Capacity to sign the basic representation agreement is based in part on the existence of mutually supportive and caring relationships.

- Adults do not lose decision-making rights even though they have appointed a representative.
- Adults can appoint whomever they want (e.g., a sister, a friend) as their representative.
- All methods of communication, both verbal and non-verbal, will be recognized.

To prevent abuse and exploitation of an adult who signs the representation agreement, a number of safeguards are available:
- All agreements must be signed in the presence of two witnesses.
- Adults must appoint a monitor to watch over the decisions of the representative.
- All agreements must be registered with the office of the Public Guardian and Trustee.
- The appointment of representatives may be challenged and the office of the Public Guardian and Trustee has the authority to investigate complaints.

NOTE The Representation Agreement Act has not yet been proclaimed, and therefore it is not yet law.

Highlights of the B.C. Guardianship Legislation

In June 1993 the B.C. government passed four new Acts comprising the new Adult Guardianship legislation in B.C. A major impetus for the new legislation was the leadership of a province-wide community-based coalition, the Adult Guardianship Coalition. While the Acts have been passed, they have not yet been proclaimed. It would therefore be premature to detail the changes expected with their implementation.

The new legislation:
- acknowledges the importance of family and friends in assisting with decision-making
- assumes that all people are capable

- validates the various methods of non-verbal communication that people use
- recognizes associate decision-makers, i.e., people who have legal status to support and assist an adult to make decisions.
- creates a representation agreement that allows people to designate representatives who will assist them to make decisions
- allows the court to appoint decision-makers for specific areas of assistance and for specific periods
- includes relationships of trust as one of the critical factors in determining a person's capacity.

income they have comes from the monthly government allowance (Disability Benefits). As such, the risk of exploitation or mismanagement is lower. Nevertheless you may wish to consider:
- joint bank accounts
- a ceiling on the amount to be withdrawn from a bank account
- joint signatures
- joint title on home ownership.

Enduring Power of Attorney
An enduring power of attorney is a written document that allows a person to confer authority upon someone else to make financial decisions on her behalf. When you confer this authority on someone else you don't lose your own authority.

The power of attorney can be revoked at any time by the

person who conferred it. There is no statutory requirement to account for the decisions made.

Conferring an enduring power of attorney is one way of establishing joint decision-making about finances. However, you do need to make sure that this power of attorney is "tailor-made" to suit your loved one's situation. It would be a good idea to seek legal advice.

NOTE that when the Representation Agreement Act is proclaimed, a representation agreement will take the place of enduring power of attorney.

Trusts
Some families establish trusts, to take effect either when they are alive, or after they have died. Consult with your lawyer and accountant as to the advantages of each arrangement. For more details, see p. 108.

PERSONAL CARE DECISIONS
This is an area of decision-making that is by far the most worrisome for most families. Adults with disabilities will likely be dealing with paid care-givers or service providers for the rest of their lives. Therefore this is the area that will have the greatest impact on their lives. Decisions that affect them are made on a constant and ongoing basis.

As parents, we want to know that our sons and daughters will have sufficient food and clothing, and that they will always have a place to live. We want to make sure that service providers and professionals do what is best. We want to make sure there is enough money to support the services and programs our sons and daughters need. Most of all, we want them to have choices, and to have those choices respected.

Fortunately, this is also the area where parents are most knowledgeable. After all, it is parents who do most of the advocating and quality assurances right now. Parents know the importance, indeed the necessity, of being vigilant. "Checking in on" is part of our job description. We know how important it is to be in regular contact with our sons and daughters and to maintain a relationship with service providers. We have a good idea of how much work this requires and how much time it takes.

Here are some options to consider in this area of decision-making:

Relationships and Personal Supports

Unfortunately no one can ever take your place. What we're looking for is the next best alternative: family members and friends. Granted, they can never replace you, but they are a natural source of assistance and the best guarantee of quality assurance. They can ensure your loved one has choices in life. They can maintain contact with service providers. They can advocate with government should the need arise. You can safeguard the future and share your expertise now with people who will be with your loved one the future.

This personal network of support will be most effective if you are clear on your vision and are able to communicate your hopes and fears, dreams and nightmares.

Advocacy

Given the limitations of the service delivery system, it is prudent to consider the role of advocates as a check and balance on the professionals involved with your son or daughter.

The best and most effective advocacy is self-advocacy by the individual involved. All other advocacy must be subservient to this principle. However, we do recognize that many people may need support and assistance to become an advocate for themselves and to advocate on their own behalf.

There are two other types of advocates. First, there are those who know your loved one and are in a relationship with him or her. They may or may not be knowledgeable about funding questions and service delivery issues. But they do know your son or daughter and will fight for their best interests.

Other advocates provide professional services. Some of these advocates are specific to the disability field. Others have a general focus and are available to everyone who is vulnerable or is a member of a minority group.

This is not a manual on advocacy. Organizations such as PLAN; the Family Support Institute; the B.C. Association for Community Living; Community Legal Assistance Society;

Advocacy

An effective advocate is someone who:

• Is free of conflict of interest.

• Is willing to visit frequently.

• Commits for the long term.

• Has credibility.

• Cares about my son or daughter.

• Has good problem-solving skills.

• Is willing to seek out and follow good advice.

• Has common sense.

• Has the time to get involved.

• Is self-confident enough not to shy away from conflict.

• Is familiar with my son or daughter's requirements.

the B.C. Coalition of People with Disabilities; and Western Family to Family are available as resources. To contact any of these groups, see Appendix, p. 149.

Micro Boards

Imagine a non-profit society that exists only to serve the program and service needs of your son or daughter. That's what a micro board is. A micro board is a small (hence the name, micro) society with a board of directors. The board of directors, usually no more than five, is comprised of committed family members and friends. This board of directors receives funding from government on behalf of the person with a disability and negotiates with service providers to provide the support services for the person. The board of directors, along with the person with a disability, direct and customize these support services.

Micro boards serve a variety of other purposes because they create opportunities for relationships of support to flourish. Overall they allow people to achieve greater control over their personal support needs. See the Appendix, p. 149, for contact information.

Individualized Funding

Most service providers receive their funding under contract from government. Often one agency or organization provides the full range of services needed by the individual. That is, they own or lease the homes, provide the staff, and offer vocational, recreational, and other support services. The result is that people who use these services often have very little say over what happens to them. Many parents and advocates are now promoting a new approach – individualized funding.

Individualized funding gives money directly to people with a disability or their representatives to enable them to purchase the particular goods and services they require. Individualized funding covers food, clothing, shelter, transportation, and technical aids as well as program and personal care supports. The individual, with the help of his or her supporters, can then determine where to live, who with, who to hire, and so on.

From first resort to last resort – joint decision-making

To ensure good decision-making for your loved one with a disability, we suggest you make the concept of joint decision-making the basis of your approach.

1. Do everything you can to enhance and validate the role of family, friends and supporters as advocates and advisors to the decisions your son or daughter makes.
2. Identify and utilize the existing advocacy system for people with disabilities.
3. Consider legal status for trusted family members or friends, such as power of attorney or joint decision-making (see box on Representation Agreements, page 83).
4. Identify people who could serve as temporary substitute decision-makers for health care decisions.
5. Consider a "committee" for specific reasons and on a time-limited basis (see note on committees, page 82).
6. Consider a "committee" only as a last resort.

There's no magic to the task of keeping people safe and respecting their choices. It's a matter of mastering the high wire. A tilt in the direction of over-protection creates a barren lifestyle. A tilt in the direction of complete autonomy without safeguards is a licence for exploitation. The risk in either direction can be minimized only when friends and family are there to care.

Unfortunately, individualized funding is not available in most communities. It is a goal to strive for. As a general principle, we believe the greater the control individuals have over their funding, the greater the choices available to them.

Conclusion: alternatives to guardianship

In this chapter we have summarized some options in preparing your son or daughter for decision-making. By now it should come as no surprise that we believe the only real protection for those you love is the people who know them and are in a relationship with them. In other words, it's the relationships that count. We look at relationships as the first resort and guardianship as the last resort. As the story at the end of this chapter suggests (What Would Happen to You? on page 89), beware of thinking that systems can be made perfect. What happened in that fictional hospital could easily happen in a group home. ■

What would happen to you?

Try this scenario on for size. You are heading to the grocery store on a beautiful sunny Saturday morning. You are a careful driver but your mind is elsewhere – on automatic pilot. Suddenly an approaching car jumps lanes and heads towards you. In a terrifying instant your life changes. After the impact you lose consciousness.

You wake up in the hospital. The pain is excruciating. You are unable to move your arms and legs. Then you discover you can't speak. A doctor and a nurse are hovering over you. They are asking a lot of questions. They want to know your blood type. You aren't able to respond. For one thing, you are in shock. For another, they aren't watching your facial gestures and you have no other way of communicating.

Now they are explaining what needs to happen to you. No one seems to notice the fear in your eyes. You hear medical terms you don't understand. You're scared and all alone. Where is your wife? Have they tried to reach her?

Suddenly you are placed on a stretcher and rushed down the hallway into an elevator, then down another hallway and into an operating room. Your last thoughts before the anesthetic takes hold are of …

Who would you think of? Your spouse, your children, your parents, your brothers and sisters, your friends?

Or your mechanic, your dentist, your lawyer?

You do survive. The hospital is crowded but they manage to find a semi-private room for you. And they locate your spouse. She comes in several hours after you return from surgery. She immediately understands your terror. You are covered with blood. The needle from the I.V. tube is already causing noticeable swelling and bruising. Your wife calls a nurse.

They respond immediately. They are cooperative and friendly. They didn't expect you to wake up so soon. The I.V. tube is adjusted and they give you a warm sponge bath. Eventually you drift off to sleep comforted by the presence of your wife. At least you are not alone.

When your wife and friends are around, you feel safer and your needs are met. They notice when you are uncomfortable. They do all the little things that make your stay tolerable.

On one occasion you had to contend with an inexperienced intern who insisted on giving you a needle in your arm even though he couldn't find a sizeable vein. You were helpless to protest. Your arm became a personal challenge to him. When a colleague from work arrived, it was bruised and bloodied. Within minutes he had your wife on the phone. She spoke to the charge nurse and a notation was made on your chart. It won't happen again, they promised. It doesn't.

What keeps you safe during your hospital stay?

Who enhances the quality of your life while you are there?

Is it the hospital policy on care? Or is it hospital rules and regulations? Is it the professional training of medical staff? Or is it nurses and doctors paid to be there?

Most of us would say we were fortunate to have friends and families to mediate the impersonal nature of the care we would receive in the hospital. They guarantee your identity. They remove the cloak of anonymity. With them you become a person again. It's not that professional paid care isn't important; it's just that you are more than the sum of your health needs. Make no mistake about it, this move from being an object of service to a real person depends on your relationships.

Why would it be any different for people with disabilities?

It isn't. However, we often make the error of assuming professional paid care is all that is necessary to keep people with disabilities safe and happy. Programs, professional supports, rules and regulations have their limitations. Paid service is not a consolation for good old-fashioned human contact, warmth and love.

It's as simple as that. Just ask anyone who has ever been in a hospital for any length of time.

I am because we are

Elizabeth Amey Kelsey Etmanski, or Liz for short, can turn a dry history assignment on New France into a love story between an Indian princess and a *coureur de bois* faster than most Grade Nine students at Hugh Boyd High.

She dreams of being a rock guitarist, idolizes Madonna, and can lip synch to most of the songs in *Wayne's World*. She can be extravagant with her make-up, prefers anything lacy, particularly those black fishnet vests, and applies something called "white mud" to her face every evening.

Boys and romance are passions she shares with her best friend Rachelle and her sisters Catherine and Theressa.

We disagree on a number of matters – her Madonna dance moves, the state of her room, the frequency of her dish washing and the need for her own phone. The latter seems an extravagance, since she has expropriated the portable one we already have, re-establishing her claim as she walks in the door. I may be off the hook, however, since she has just seen the perfect electric guitar. It's bright red and costs "only $450, Dad."

She earns the occasional detention, would rather catch a video than do homework, and has a wicked sense of humour, especially about my bald spot. Notwithstanding, she is an adornment to her dad's life, equal in beauty and charm to both her younger and older sisters.

Yet there is a darkness already threatening a corner of her future. Not that Liz is aware, fortunately. She sees the world as Timothy Findley describes it, "whole and green and alive with promise." The spectre sadly is all mine.

In four years she begins a high stakes game of chance. On her 19th birthday the law will silently confer the assumption of decision-making capability on Liz. It is a Pandora's present.

The standards of decision-making capability in our society remain firmly rooted in a narrowly defined, highly overrated form of intellectual ability. In our province the legal test is your ability to demonstrate you understand the nature and effect of your decision.

Using that standard, Liz, who has Down's syndrome, would most likely fail.

The utensils the law has to measure our worth have not changed significantly throughout this century. Neither has their intent. Verbal ability, proficiency of expression and abstract intellectual thinking remain the criteria for determining a person's decision-making ability.

As long as our society continues to ignore other factors that contribute to decision-making, there is no equality in the assumption of capability; there is intellectual imperialism. IQ scores may have faded from use but their successors haven't. The law has embraced them all.

We know, learn, and understand even when we cannot explain. We learn through self-awareness, through our relationships and through confronting the challenges of our environment. We can know emotionally, spiritually, and intuitively. We can express ourselves through the medium of music, art, mathematics, relationships, and love. Our tears, laughter, smiles and frowns reveal our trust, confidence, security and wishes as surely as intellectual expression.

Ask yourself how you have made some of the important decisions in your life. Marriage? Children? Change of career? New car? Can you honestly say you understood the consequences of your decisions all the time?

How often did you rationalize afterward? And how often did you make decisions alone, completely cut off from advice, consultation or influence of any kind? Is there really such a thing as independent decision-making?

Our insights into the varied, complex and different ways of knowing remain half-eaten, too strange and threatening to be digested by the law. Its teeth are clenched. Liz and her abilities are a forbidden delicacy.

As an adult Liz can anticipate the law ignoring her decision-making ability and ultimately usurping it. The law does not value her intuition, her compassion, her manner of expression and her relationships.

As a father I am beset by burning questions. Which benign agents of society's institutions will challenge Liz's decisions? What choices and risks will they eliminate from her life under the guise of protection? How will the mask of caring prevent her initiation into life's mysteries.

When the law demands the password of her, will it appreciate the determination that convinced the largest bookstore in North America to search for an hour for a book on signing which she didn't know the title of? She knew it when she saw it.

Will it value her diplomatic skills, mature enough to find common ground even in irreconcilable positions? Will it honour her ability to assess emotions with uncanny accuracy and to read a room with more facility than any politician? Will it credit her storytelling, her humour, and her razor-sharp imitations of friends and family? Will it understand her motivation to plough through babysitting and leadership training courses even though she is just learning to read?

My daughter has a wisdom that eludes many of us. She understands her limitations and adjusts with patience and eagerness. She negotiates the complexities and inequities of her world with more ingenuity, courage and equanimity than she should have to. She offers, for all those willing to listen, a course in perfecting a life.

Yet, unlike her sisters, Liz is a candidate for exclusion.

No admittance. Access forbidden. Restricted. Off limits. Too risky. Vulnerable. Incompetence. Choices ignored. For your own good. Go directly to … a program, a service, a professional, an institution, a legal guardian. Become a client, not a citizen.

Our province, like many jurisdictions in North America, is currently reviewing its guardianship legislation. We need laws that recognize Liz's talents and attitudes, including her ability to participate in caring, committed and trusting relationships. That's really what keeps you and me safe and contributes to the quality of our decisions.

If that kind of brilliance were to shine on the darkened corner of Liz's future, I know an Indian princess and a *coureur de bois* who would be pleased.

AL ETMANSKI

Worksheet 5

JOINT DECISION-MAKING

Use this worksheet to organize your joint decision-making choices. We suggest you fill out the checklist first, then record the information about your son or daughter's decision-making.

A. Checklist

MEDICAL DECISION-MAKING

☐ YES ☐ NO   I have discussed issues of medical consent with my loved one's doctor.

☐ YES ☐ NO   The doctor accepts consent from my son or daughter for medical treatment.

☐ YES ☐ NO   The doctor accepts my consent for medical care on his or her behalf.

FINANCIAL DECISION-MAKING

☐ YES ☐ NO   I have set up an income trust.

☐ YES ☐ NO   I have set up a discretionary trust.

☐ YES ☐ NO   My son or daughter has a bank account.

☐ YES ☐ NO   Withdrawals from that bank account are protected by:
- joint signature for withdrawals
- my son or daughter is well known to bank employees
- funds in the account are kept to a minimum

☐ YES ☐ NO   I have set up an enduring power of attorney.

PERSONAL CARE DECISION-MAKING

☐ YES ☐ NO My son or daughter has an advocate.

☐ YES ☐ NO The services s/he receives are monitored by a separate and independent agency.

☐ YES ☐ NO Housing supports are kept separate from other services.

☐ YES ☐ NO Staff understand and support the importance of family involvement.

☐ YES ☐ NO Staff understand and welcome the involvement of friends and members of the personal network.

☐ YES ☐ NO Service and program staff recognize the importance of offering and respecting my loved one's choices.

☐ YES ☐ NO Families and friends provide support by reviewing services and programs on a regular basis. (**NOTE** This is different from the service plans developed by service providers.)

B. Information

GENERAL

Who does my son or daughter trust? _____

_____

_____

Who would I trust to assist my loved one with decision-making? _____

_____

_____

_____

Who understands my loved one's communication style? _____

_____

_____

_____

MEDICAL DECISIONS

Who is my son or daughter's doctor? _____

What assistance would my loved one need to make medical decisions?

_____

_____

_____

Who would I and my loved one accept to assist with medical decision-making?

_____

_____

What aspect of their medical care do I think my loved one might understand?

_____

_____

_____

What formal arrangements do I need to make to ensure medical care is easily

available to my son or daughter? _____

_____

_____

_____

FINANCIAL DECISIONS

My son or daughter's trustees are: _____

_____

_____

S/he has a bank account at: _____

_____

PERSONAL CARE DECISIONS

My son or daughter's advocate is: _____

The independent agency that monitors services is: _____

_____

Friends and families review services and programs at these intervals:

_____

Developing *your* Will and Estate Plan

You can never do a
kindness too soon,
because you never
know how soon it
will be too late.

EMERSON

What the heck, it can't hurt me

"A LOT OF PEOPLE my age have thought about this problem for most of their adult life. They hope their plans are adequate. Maybe they made a will 30 years ago. Or maybe they hope that magically new plans will come together at the last minute. I don't think that's good enough.

"When you have a child with a disability you get lots of advice. But usually nothing ever materializes. So you get kind of negative. However you have to remember that every once in a while something comes along and it does work.

"I knew if I was going to make progress I had to take chances. What the heck, I said, it can't hurt me."

George's involvement with other parents associated with PLAN encouraged him to think about where he was going and what he wanted to achieve. "I call it putting your house in order. They got me moving but you have to be willing to do it. It means getting organized — getting all your necessary papers together.

"My original will is long gone. We made a new one just before my wife died. I changed it a year later to include some clauses I heard about from other families. Then I decided to change my trustee and to include a role for PLAN after I died. So I got another lawyer and she drafted a new will. It's never really over, you know. If I find out about something better and I'm still around I'll make changes again. Actually, altering your will is easy and not that expensive. Things are evolving and you are bound to get new ideas.

"My first goal was to make sure there were sufficient funds to look after Rick. I got advice on prescribed insured annuities and how to use life insurance to increase the size of my estate. There were things about life insurance I never appreciated. I just about doubled the size of my estate with one financial decision. And the money would be available for Rick immediately after I died. It wouldn't be tied up in probate and it wouldn't be taxable.

"These were the sorts of things I knew nothing about. The fact that other parents were exploring the same things gave me confidence."

George also decided to change trust companies. He thought they all were the same – straight business operations. Then he heard through the "parent grapevine" about a company that went the extra mile. In fact after the death of one parent, the trust officer made arrangements for the memorial service, bringing his kettle to the reception after. He helped the son with a disability move and now stays in regular contact, not only with the son but also with his Personal Network. George wanted that kind of service for Rick so he shifted companies.

"I didn't figure I could take my previous trust officer out to lunch. Or for that matter that he would ever be interested in taking Rick out to lunch. I wanted a more personal approach and I got it."

continued on page 102

Developing Your Will and Estate Plan

Our purpose in this chapter is to provide general information about wills, and suggest tools to use when you are considering estate planning for someone with a disability. The information in this chapter will:

- explain some of the issues involved in preparing a will when one of the beneficiaries has a disability;
- urge you to consult with a lawyer who is familiar with these issues and who will help you draft a valid will; and
- explain how you need to revisit your will periodically, and update it when necessary.

This chapter won't replace the need to make some tough choices. It means leaving the path that, for many of us, is too well trodden – the path of least resistance. Your will and estate plan is the tool or the implement or the vehicle that you will use. It is not a substitute for your actual wishes. The will and estate plan is the only technical part of the future planning process. The rest is all art.

This chapter highlights major points about will and estate planning. It does not cover everything. When you are preparing a will that includes your wishes for a child with a disability, it is essential to get legal advice.

In praise of the imperfect will

You've heard the facts before. Too many people either die without a will or with a will that's out-of-date. You want to avoid joining their ranks. But you don't have all the answers. You still need to work out a few more details. You're just about there. Maybe after reading this chapter!

Well, we're sorry to disappoint you. This chapter will not help you create the perfect will. Neither will any other book. Or person, for that matter. So don't make the same mistake too many others have done. Don't wait for something that will never happen.

GEORGE'S STORY
continued from page 100

For George the company of other
families helped get him moving. Looking
back on it now he realizes how easy it
really was. The time spent was negligible
compared to the time he had spent
worrying. ■

> **Worksheet 6 – Will Planning for Parents of Children and Adults with Disabilities**
>
> This worksheet will help you clarify your objectives in making a will. The worksheet is located at the back of this section, on p.116. Take a look at it now. Before you make decisions about your will, fill out this worksheet in detail. It will save lots of time later.

Now is the time to develop and execute the "imperfect" will. We feel so strongly about this we might call our next book, *In Praise of Imperfection.*

What's so great about perfection anyway? Where did we get the grandiose illusion that we humans can either be perfect or get things perfect? Surely that's the job of divine personalities, beyond the scope of mere mortals. True, our culture seems to value athletic achievement and intellectual prowess – if you are to believe the advertisers. Few, if any of us, ever attain these standards. Yet we still manage to get on with our lives.

And that's what we want you to do with your will. Get on with it! Preparing and executing the "imperfect" will is not the least you can do, it's the best you can do.

> Do not fear mistakes.
> There are none.
> MILES DAVIS

Beginning to create your will

Before you create your will, you need to be clear about the details. Every family situation is unique. You are going to rely on your family after you are gone, so it's a good idea to discuss things with your family.

There are other valuable resource people you might consider talking to: extended family and friends, members of your son or daughter's personal network, and members of your church congregation, if you have one.

In our experience parents have often been able to clarify their objectives by talking to others. The more open and forthright your discussions are, the clearer your objectives will be.

Seven key objectives

Most people want their will and estate plan to:
1. Pay their debts, taxes, and other liabilities.
2. Provide a separate independent income for their spouse.
3. Distribute their assets according to their wishes.
4. Maximize the size of their estate for their children.
5. Protect the estate of their son or daughter with a disability.
6. Ensure that there is a guardian for their children under 19.
7. Avoid delays, family strife, needless taxation, costly legal challenges, probate fees and government involvement.

Basic questions about wills

Once you've added your own personalized objectives to the general objectives described above and you are comfortable (well, reasonably comfortable) with your answers, you are ready for the technical solutions. Here are some questions and answers to start you on your way.

NOTE For a complete list of legal terms, see "Demystifying definitions that could definitely derail you", on page 115.

WHAT IS A WILL?
A will is the legal document that tells people what to do with your estate. It helps makes life easier for those left behind by providing a plan for them to follow.

WHAT ARE THE BASIC THINGS I NEED TO THINK ABOUT?
During the course of designing your will you will need to:
- Appoint an executor to ensure that the instructions in your will are carried out
- Divide your estate among family (spouse and children), charities and others. A person who inherits or receives part of your estate is called a beneficiary.
- Create a trust, usually a discretionary trust, for your child or relative with a disability and identify a trustee and perhaps co-trustee to manage the trust.
- Appoint a guardian for your children who are under 19.

Is your child under 19?

If you have young children and you die without a will, here's what happens.

ONE If there is a surviving spouse he/she gets the first $65,000 of the estate, plus the household furnishings and the right to live in the family home until his/her death. Your estate will be divided according to the Estate Administration Act.

• The remainder of the estate is divided as follows: one-third to the surviving spouse and the balance divided equally between any children.

• The funds for your children will be held in trust by the Public Trustee until your children reach the age of majority.

• The surviving spouse will have to apply to the Public Trustee's office to access the money held in trust for the use, maintenance and benefit of the child(ren). This holds true for day-to-day expenses as well as any special expenditures.

TWO If there is no surviving parent (that is, you both die) or there is no surviving parent who has legal custody, the Superintendent of Family and Child Services becomes the guardian of the person, and the Public Trustee becomes guardian of their estate. In order for another relative or family friend to become guardian, they will have to apply to the B.C. Supreme Court.

To prevent a costly, complicated and potentially messy and heartbreaking outcome, you must make a will.

WHY DO I NEED A WILL?

If you die without a will, the Estate Administration Act sets out how your estate will be distributed. Under this Act the court will appoint an administrator who will divide your estate. You will have no control over how your estate is divided. You will not be able to protect the inheritance you want to leave to your son or daughter with a disability. S/he may be disqualified from receiving Disability Benefits.

If you die without a will and you have children who are under the age of 19, and there is no surviving parent who is the legal guardian, the government will become guardian of those children.

WHAT HAPPENS IF I DIE WITHOUT A WILL?

If you die without a will, the B.C. Estate Administration Act directs how your estate will be dealt with:

- the first $65,000 of your property goes to your spouse, plus the household furnishings, and the right to live in the family home until death;
- one third of the remainder of your estate goes to your spouse and the remaining two thirds is divided equally among your children;
- your next-of-kin will have to go to court to get authority to deal with your estate; and
- the Public Trustee will likely become committee of the estate for your adult child with a disability.

WHAT OTHER LAWS AND REGULATIONS DO I NEED TO KNOW ABOUT WHEN I'M PLANNING MY WILL?

The Wills Variation Act

This Act requires that you provide adequately for your spouse and your children. If a spouse or children feel you have not provided adequately for them in your will, they can ask the court to change your will to get a larger share of the estate. This must be done within 6 months of probate.

The Public Trustee Act and the Estate Administration Act

The Public Trustee is responsible for protecting the interests of children who are under 19 or dependent adults. Your executor is required to send a copy of your will to the Public Trustee after you die if you have children under 19 or an adult child who is or may be "mentally infirm." The Public Trustee will examine the will to see if you have made adequate provision for your children under 19 or your adult child with a disability. If you have not done so, the Public Trustee may contest your will on their behalf.

Disability Benefits from B.C. Benefits

Disability Benefits is a provincial government plan. It provides financial support, and medical and health benefits to people with disabilities who are unable to work because of their disability and cannot support themselves.

Once people are 18 years of age, they are entitled to Disability Benefits from B.C. Benefits if:

- They qualify as a person with disabilities under the rules in the Disability Benefits Program Act and regulations.

- They have less than $3,000 in assets. Assets are things a person owns. Assets include things such as money, property or investments.

NOTE Some assets, for example, a house which a person owns and lives in or a car, do not affect a person's right to Disability Benefits.

These are substantial benefits. At the time of writing, the benefits include an allowance up to $771 per month, a bus pass for one year for $45, and medical, dental, optical and pharmaceutical coverage.

The Disability Benefits Program Act, regulations, and policy change from time to time. Check what the current situation is.

HOW ARE DISABILITY BENEFITS AFFECTED BY INCOME SUCH AS AN INHERITANCE?

If people on Disability Benefits receive money from an inheritance, a life insurance payout, an ICBC payout, or other financial windfall, up to $100,000 can be placed in a trust and treated as an exempt asset. This means that the person's Disability Benefits are not affected. The $100,000 can be placed in a "non-discretionary trust" and disbursements from the trust can be used for that person's benefit.

The Director of B.C. Benefits has the discretion to exempt an amount higher than the $100,000 if the disability-related costs will be higher.

NOTE While there is a ceiling of $100,000 for non-discretionary trusts, there is no ceiling for discretionary trusts. See the next page.

Earned income is treated differently. A person on Disability Benefits is allowed to keep the first $200 and 25% of the rest up to $5,484 a year. This is called the enhanced earnings exemption.

If you do not leave your child with a disability (either an adult child or a minor) a fair share of your estate, it is likely the Public Trustee will intervene on the child's behalf and try to change the will.

HOW CAN I MAKE A WILL THAT
IS BEST FOR A CHILD WITH A DISABILITY?

You can set up a trust in your will for the person with a disability. The best course of action is to talk to a lawyer who has expertise in providing wills and estate advice to families of people with disabilities.

There are two common trusts used by families of people with disabilities: non-discretionary trusts, which are also called income trusts, and discretionary trusts.

Non-Discretionary Trusts

In a non-discretionary trust, also called an income trust, your beneficiary gets a certain amount of money at regular times. For example, your child might get $600 each month. It is up to you to decide how much money will be paid to the beneficiary and at what times.

An non-discretionary trust is usually set up when the parents know the child will not need Disability Benefits in the future.

Discretionary Trusts

Most families of people with disabilities choose to set up a discretionary trust in their will. You appoint a trustee (and possibly a co-trustee) in your will as the person who will be in charge of the trust. You give the trustee the discretion, or power, to decide when and how much of the trust fund will be used for the beneficiary, in this case your child or relative with a disability. Your trustee can gauge your loved one's changing needs from time to time.

HOW DOES A DISCRETIONARY TRUST
AFFECT MY LOVED ONE?

A discretionary trust allows the person to continue to receive Disability Benefits. The trustee will buy your loved one what is needed. Your child or relative is not allowed to demand any of the assets of the trust. This means s/he cannot be said to have assets greater than $3,000.

Under B.C. Benefits, discretionary trusts are recognized as an exempt asset. There is no ceiling on the amount that can

be placed in a discretionary trust. The trustee can use the trust for such things as:
- medical aids and devices, renovation, education and training, cost of caregivers, etc., plus
- expenses of up to $5,484 a year that promote independence.

The trustee could check with PLAN to make sure s/he has current information about these rules.

WHAT HAPPENS TO THE MONEY LEFT IN THE TRUST WHEN THE BENEFICIARY DIES?

When you set up a trust in a will for a beneficiary, you must also state in the will who will get what is left in the trust when the beneficiary dies. This could be children, siblings, other family members, charities etc.

In choosing whom the money will go to you should be careful to avoid a conflict of interest. The person responsible for spending the money on behalf of the person with a disability should not be the person receiving the money when the beneficiary dies.

If a clear conflict of interest occurs in a will, the Public Trustee may try to alter the will.

WHAT DOES A TRUSTEE DO?

The trustee:
- manages, or looks after, the trust assets; and
- makes sure your child or relative receives trust benefits according to your wishes.

If you decide to set up a trust for your child or relative you will need to name the trustee in your will. Choosing a trustee is one of the most crucial decisions you will make about future planning. The person you choose may have responsibilities as a trustee for 40 years or more. It is a good idea to have more than one trustee. For example, you may want to have two trustees and two alternates, in case the original trustees cannot act or cannot agree.

WHO SHOULD BE A TRUSTEE?

You may want to have a financial trustee and a personal trustee. Their skills may be different and may complement

All flesh is grass and all its beauty is like the flowers of the field. The grass withers, the flower fades, when the breath of the Lord blows upon it.

ISAIAH 40:6-7

each other. One may be a good investment money manager and may keep accounts, manage tax returns etc. The other could be in close personal contact with the beneficiary and know what to spend money on.

You may consider using a respected trust company as one of the trustees. Some parents use a trust company as one trustee and a relative or family friend as the other trustee. The trust company can make sure there is experienced financial help to manage the trust. The relative or family friend should have a personal interest in your loved one but must not be in a conflict of interest.

If you name a person as a trustee you should also name a successor in case that person dies or moves or is not willing to continue. It is best if the trustees are people your child or relative knows and likes. The trustees and your loved one will likely be involved with one another for a long time. A good relationship between them will benefit everyone.

At least one of the trustees should live close to your loved one. If a trustee has close contact with your child or relative, they will understand their needs better.

WHAT ARE THE DUTIES OF A TRUSTEE?
The duties of a trustee include:
- exercising discretion to release funds when necessary
- providing investment management of assets
- coordinating any maintenance/repairs of real estate
- preparing trust tax returns
- maintaining records of the trust

DO TRUSTEES GET PAID IN B.C.?
Yes, trustees are paid a fee from the estate. Your beneficiaries or the court must approve the fee. The Trustee Act currently states that the maximum fees for executors are:
- Capital fee not exceeding 5% of the estate.
- Income fee not exceeding 5% of the income collected per annum.
- Trust management fee of 0.4% of the capital of the trust per annum.

Every time
we say,
Let there be!
in any form,
something
happens.
STELLA TERRILL MANN

CAN I APPOINT A GUARDIAN FOR MY CHILD IN MY WILL?

If you have children under age 19 you should appoint a guardian for them in your will. You should also appoint alternates in case the first are not able to accept. You can't appoint a guardian for an adult child even if the child is severely handicapped. Guardians for adults can only be appointed by a court and are called committees.

WHAT INVESTMENT POWERS SHOULD I GIVE MY TRUSTEE?

Trustees are limited by law to very conservative and safe investments. In your will, you may give them broader investment powers. For example, you may wish them to have the power to buy an apartment for your child to live in. Be sure to discuss this with your lawyer.

WHO SHOULD BE THE EXECUTOR OF MY WILL?

The executor is the person who makes sure that the instructions in your will are carried out after you die. Normally you appoint your spouse as your executor, but you may need to appoint someone else. You should then appoint alternates.

If you have set up a trust in your will, usually the executor and alternate executor will be the same as your trustees and alternate trustees. However, in some cases, for example where there is business to be managed, you may wish to have different executors and trustees. Talk to your lawyer about this.

WHICH OF MY ASSETS DO NOT FORM PART OF MY ESTATE AND PASS OUTSIDE THE WILL?

Any assets held in joint tenancy with another person pass directly to that person on your death and are not governed by your will. For example, a home and bank accounts held in joint tenancy with your spouse go directly to your spouse on your death.

Life insurance policies with a designated adult beneficiary pass outside the will directly to that beneficiary.

RRSPs and RRIFs with a designated beneficiary pass directly to that beneficiary.

Quite often when a spouse dies, most of the family assets are held in one of these ways and pass directly to the surviving spouse. Assets which pass outside your will save probate fees.

Be sure to consult your lawyer about putting assets in joint tenancy with your children as there are dangers as well as benefits in so doing.

WHAT IS PROBATE?

Probate is the name of the legal process that confirms your will. Normally it is the job of your executor to file for probate with the provincial court. This process can be quite lengthy (up to about six months). Until your executor receives the grant of probate, assets of your estate cannot be released.

Probate fees in B.C. are currently as follows:

- Under $10,000   No fee
- $10,000-$25,000 $200
- $25,000-$50,000 $6 for each $1,000
- Over $50,000 $14 for each $1,000

Seeking advice from professionals

There are a variety of experienced professionals in the future planning business. There is no substitute for good professional help. There are lawyers, financial planners, accountants and trust offices who have special expertise in helping plan for the needs of children and relatives with disabilities. They can help you maximize the size of your estate, save you money, and ensure that your instructions are written in proper legal language. They are guided by principles of confidentiality, prudent administration and sound judgment.

As with all professional services, be a cautious consumer. Ask other parents or check with organizations such as PLAN that are working on behalf of people with disabilities or their families. PLAN can provide some sample clauses that you may want to include in your will.

Resources

As you begin to draw up your will, you will find the following materials useful. Both are available from PLAN.

• Wills and Estates: Planning for Parents and Families of Persons with a Disability. A brochure prepared by the People's Law School.

• Will and Estate Kit. Produced and distributed by PLAN.

The professional who advises you may refer to "wills and estate planning." This is a term we often hear, but what exactly does estate planning mean?

Estate planning is quite a broad term. It includes such things as:

• preparing your will
• reviewing the need for powers of attorney
• deciding upon issues such as executor and trustee appointment, and finding ways to minimize probate fees
• calculating your estate needs and determining the amount of life insurance needed to meet those needs
• looking at strategies to reduce income taxes at death

Life changes

No matter how exhaustive your preparation and thorough your study, your will may never be complete. While preparing for this chapter we were consulting with one of the most prestigious estate planners in the country. He interrupted our interview to visit his lawyer. After over thirty-five years in the business he was still revising his will.

Expect to revise your will as life changes. The act of revision is relatively painless and inexpensive. And the peace of mind is incalculable. ∎

Six tips to making your will if you have a child with a disability

1. Complete the Will Planning Worksheet accurately. This will give you an idea of your assets, and help you make decisions.
2. Decide how you want your estate distributed (e.g. all to wife and when she dies, split among children in equal shares).
3. Decide if you want to set up a discretionary trust for your child with a disability. If you do, decide who will be:
   - the trustee of the discretionary trust
   - the beneficiary of the trust when your child dies

   Ensure there is no conflict of interest.
4. Be aware that the following pass outside the will:
   - life insurance with a designated beneficiary
   - RRSPs and RRIFs with a designated beneficiary
   - assets held in joint tenancy

   You may wish to use some of these provisions.
5. If you have children under 19 years of age, decide whom you will appoint as their guardian.
6. Take all this information to a lawyer who has experience in wills and estates for people who have children with disabilities. Ask the lawyer to explain the tax and legal implications of your decisions. Also ask the lawyer about registering the will, once it has been drawn up.

Demystifying definitions that could definitely derail you

Beneficiary - a person to whom you leave things (money, gifts, insurance policy, RRSP, trust).

Bequest - A gift of a specific item of personal property or a specific amount of cash identified in your will.

Codicil - A legal document used to amend portions of your original will and requiring the same formalities of signing and witnessing needed for a will.

Discretionary trust - A trust in which the choice as to how to spend the interest and principal is completely in the hands of the trustee.

Enduring Power of Attorney - The power to conduct and manage your financial affairs even if you become incapable. See Power of Attorney.

Executor - The person or professional named in the will who is responsible for ensuring the wishes in your will are carried out.

Grant of Probate - This is the executor's proof they can act as your executor.

Intestate - A person who dies intestate dies without a valid will.

Inter Vivos Trust - A trust that comes into effect during the lifetime of the person who established the trust. Also known as a Living Trust.

Life Interest - Benefit given to someone in a will which allows that person to have the use of the property or a certain sum of money only for the lifetime of that person.

Non Probatable Assets - Assets that pass outside of the will. For example joint tenant ownership of real estate and bank accounts, RRSP/RRIF, life insurance and annuity beneficiaries.

Power of Attorney - A written document giving someone else the authority to make financial and legal decisions on your behalf. Often used if you are going to be out of the country or want help in dealing with your financial affairs. See Enduring Power of Attorney.

Probate - The procedure by which the will of the deceased person is legally approved by the court and documented. It also confirms the appointment of your Executor.

Revocation - Cancelling parts of or all of an existing will.

Settlor - The individual who establishes a trust.

Testator - That's you, the person who makes the will.

Testamentary Trust - A trust set up in a will that only takes effect after your death.

Trust - A legal arrangement in which one person (the settlor) transfers legal title to a Trustee to manage the property for the benefit of a person or institution (the beneficiaries).

Trustee - The person or company that manages the trust according to the instructions in the trust agreement or will.

Worksheet 6

WILL PLANNING FOR PARENTS OF CHILDREN AND ADULTS WITH DISABILITIES

This worksheet is intended to:
- Assist you in compiling information to take to your lawyer when you wish to make your will.
- Assist in making you aware of decisions you will need to make and to help you make them.

After completing the worksheet you will be ready to contact a lawyer of your choice to make the will.

A. Personal and Family Particulars

Date _____

1 Full Name _____

Address _____

_____

Occupation _____

Home Phone _____   Office Phone _____

Date of Birth _____   Place of Birth _____

Citizenship _____

Marital Status (including plans to marry) _____

Date of Marriage _____ Place of Marriage _____

Do you have a marriage contract? _____

Have you or your spouse been married before? _____

2 Spouse's Full Name _____

Address _____

_____

Occupation _____

Home Phone _____ Office Phone _____

Date of Birth _____ Place of Birth _____

Citizenship _____

If you are not married, do you have a common law partner? _____

If so, who? _____

3 Children (Please note any child of a former marriage of either spouse and any child with a disability.)

Full Name   Date of Birth

_____   _____

_____   _____

_____   _____

_____   _____

_____   _____

B. Will Particulars

1 a) Do you wish to leave the residue of your estate to your spouse if he/she survives

you? _____

b) If your spouse fails to survive you, do you wish to leave your estate to your

children? _____

c) What share do you wish each child to get? Equal shares? _____

If unequal, please specify who gets what. _____

_____

_____

_____

d) If your children are minors, at what age do you wish them to receive their share

of your estate? _____

e) If any child dies before you, what do you want to happen to his/her share of your

estate? _____

_____

_____

2 a) Do you wish to set up a trust for anyone?

   b) If so, who? _____

   c) Do you wish the trust to be a discretionary trust? _____

   d) Who do you wish to be trustees/executors of the trust?

Name (in full) _____

Address _____

_____

Relationship to you _____

Occupation _____

   e) Who will be alternate trustees?

Name (in full) _____

Address _____

_____

Relationship to you _____

Occupation _____

Name (in full) _____

Address _____

_____

Relationship to you _____

Occupation _____

f) Who do you wish to receive the money left in the trust when the person for whom the trust was set up dies?

   (i) the person's spouse _____

   (ii) the person's children _____

   (iii) others? _____

g) Is there a possible conflict of interest? _____

3 a) Who do you wish as guardian(s) to your children who are under 19 years of age?

Name (in full) _____

Address _____

_____

Relationship to you _____

Occupation _____

b) Who will be alternate guardians?

Name (in full) _____

Address _____

_____

Relationship to you _____

Occupation _____

4 Do you have any specific articles you wish to give to any particular person (s)?

Name (in full) _____

ITEM _____

Name (in full) _____

ITEM _____

Name (in full) _____

ITEM _____

Name (in full) _____

ITEM _____

5 Do you have any cash gifts you wish to make to any relatives or charities or _____ ?

Name (in full) _____

Address _____

_____

Relationship to you _____

Occupation _____

AMOUNT _____

Name (in full) _____

Address _____

_____

Relationship to you _____

Occupation _____

AMOUNT _____

Name (in full) _____

Address _____

_____

Relationship to you _____

Occupation _____

AMOUNT _____

Name (in full) _____

Address _____

Relationship to you _____

Occupation _____

AMOUNT _____

6 a) Do you wish to give your trustee power to buy, sell, or hold mortgages on property in which your child lives? _____

b) What investment powers do you wish to give your trustee? You may wish to discuss this with your lawyer or financial advisor. Note that the investments trustees can make are limited by law and are conservative.

_____

_____

_____

7 Do you wish Planned Lifetime Advocacy Network (PLAN) to provide support to your child when you are no longer able to do so? _____

If so, contact PLAN to discuss incorporating appropriate clauses into your will that will enable PLAN to assist your loved one.

C. Other

1 Do you own property outside British Columbia? _____

_____

2 Have you been married prior to your present marriage? _____

3 Are you living common law? _____

4 Other comments or instructions _____

_____

_____

_____

_____

_____

THIS WORKSHEET IS ADAPTED FROM MATERIAL DEVELOPED BY DAVIS & CO.

Securing *your* Plan

Let the beauty of what we
love be what we do. There
are hundreds of ways to
kneel and kiss the ground.

RUMI, 13TH CENTURY

Back seat driver

GEORGE HALL has seen the future and he likes what he sees. Sure he still has worries, but he is satisfied he has done everything he can think of to ensure Rick's future. What's more, he has seen Rick thrive in his new life. George has a real sense of what will happen when he's not around.

He has already started to take a back seat in his son's life. "I'm seventy-three next month," he exclaims. "I'm slowing down a bit. I guess I've earned the right to be a back-seat driver."

Besides, George has a backup. The chauffeur for all his plans is, no surprise, PLAN. He has signed a full membership contract with PLAN. PLAN is prepared to make a lifetime commitment to monitor the quality of Rick's life, to maintain the health of Rick's "circle," to provide advice to the trustee, to visit Rick on a regular basis, and to stay on top of all the other plans George has made. In other words, all the things that parents do for their children now, PLAN is prepared to do after they're gone.

In this regard PLAN spells continuity as well as relief to George. "It's better to make your arrangements with a group that you expect to be around for a while," he concludes.

But there's more. You see, while it's true that George's plans for Rick are focused on Rick's future, they are really about George's future as well.

George is selling the family home, leaving Rick behind and moving to Sechelt on the Sunshine Coast. That's a move he never would have considered in the past.

George's wisdom is astute. "Part of the enrichment in life is learning. If you're feeling at all uncomfortable about your plans, a few simple steps will enhance the future for both you and your loved one. You can't depend on anybody else, the government, the local association, your friends or family, on a loose arrangement."

As a former salmon fisheries biologist, George knows a lot about swimming upstream, about enhancement, about courage and about destiny. It's time, he thinks, to complete the life cycle.

Besides you can't really qualify as a back-seat driver without having been in the driver's seat first. ∎

Securing Your Plan

Introduction

By now you are probably convinced that planning a secure future requires careful attention to a number of elements:
- the continuing involvement of caring, committed friends and family
- control over the home environment
- a properly drawn and executed will
- a sizeable discretionary trust
- sensitive and caring trustees

You will have thought about:
- how you want to divide your property
- whether to establish a discretionary trust
- which company or relative or friend might be a trustee or co-trustee of the discretionary trust
- what services you may want from a lawyer, trust officer and financial planner

You have a clearer idea about what your child's life will be like after you are gone:
- who their friends will be
- where they might live
- what might be put in place to keep them safe
- who might serve as an advocate and monitor
- what role your other children and family members might play

Searching for guarantees in an uncertain future

If you are like us, you may still have concerns. Here are some that keep coming back to haunt us:
- What keeps all the components of the Personal Future Plan functioning and connected after you are gone?

- Who watches over the people and institutions you are depending on?
- What if something unexpected happens?
- Who will be your eyes, ears, arms and legs when you are no longer around?

As long as you are around you can pick up the pieces if things do not work out. You are the one who notices when something is wrong. That, by definition, is what moms and dads are meant to do, isn't it? You have nurtured and sweated to create a good life for your loved one. But unless you have access to special privileges unavailable to the rest of us, you won't be around forever.

You will not be able to see the results of your Personal Future Plan. Your challenge – to make arrangements for a safe, secure and comfortable life well into the future, perhaps as long as another fifty or sixty years – is immense. Who knows what the future will be like?

Flowers and compost

When you think of it, a parent's job description is much like a gardener's. To nurture, to hover, to be alert to changing conditions, to provide shelter from the storm, to fertilize where appropriate, to enjoy all stages of growth, to savour the beauty of the moment and to appreciate the sweat of preparation. You learn a lot about life as a gardener. You learn, for instance, about the inter-relationship between flowers and compost.

A beautiful rose that we have just cut and placed in our vase is very pure. It smells so good, fresh and fragrant. Rotting compost is the opposite. It reeks and is full of decomposing garbage, slime and filth.

But that is only if we look on the surface. If we look more closely, we will see that in five or six days the rose will become part of the compost. The truth is, we do not need to wait that long. We can see it now. Take a deep look at the rose. Can you see the compost in the rose? Take another look at the compost. Can you see the rose in the compost? Can you see its contents transformed in a few months into lovely vegetables, maybe even into another beautiful rose?

If you are a gardener, you recognize the interrelationship between the beautiful flower and the rotting compost. You cannot have one without the other. They need each other. The rose and the compost are equal. The compost is just as precious as the rose.

If you are a parent you understand that much of the beauty you create arises out of life's darker moments or in response to threats on the horizon. This is true for our children. It is also true for us as a grouping of families. The parent-based disability movement arose at the end of the Second World War in the wake of the eugenics movement and the horrible atrocities committed against people with disabilities, and in reaction to professional advice to send our children away to institutions. Those early seeds of change, planted in dank soil, have blossomed into the most wondrous of plants. The parent-based disability movement was the first internationally-based consumer movement. Before Ralph Nader, before consumerism, we existed!

We've done it before and we may have to do it again. We don't pretend to have a crystal ball. Nevertheless we see some disturbing trends on the horizon. At the very least they deserve a sober second thought. Think of them as the climatic conditions that any sensible gardener needs to be aware of. So let's descend underground into the compost and poke around for a while. Perhaps we'll see the beginning of another beautiful plant!

Disturbing trends

Parents know how to turn adversity around: to create beauty out of ugliness; to see the rose in the compost. In preparing for a safe and secure future for our children, we need to understand the "composting" part. Facing what's out there with open eyes is a prudent response, wouldn't you say? At the moment, what's out there are a number of trends that alarm us.

FUNDING CUTBACKS

If your son or daughter is dependent on services delivered or funded by government, then the availability and quality of these programs are dependent on the future health of provincial and national economies. Access to these services is also dependent on political priorities and political commitment. While provincial governments have a statutory responsibility to fund disability assistance and supports for children, there is no guarantee of the quality. The federal government's commitment to funding provincial social services is declining. Many analysts worry that national standards for the quality of these programs will also decline. Finally, provincial governments have no statutory responsibility to fund adult services, let alone maintain them at their current level of quality.

RATIONING OF HEALTH CARE

Governments talk openly about the high costs of health care. They discuss introducing "user fees." Long waiting lists already exist for elective surgery, for cancer treatment, for heart operations. Hospitals and doctors are already making "triage" decisions about who will receive medical treatment and who will have to wait. Can people with disabilities be assured of fair access to medical treatment in the future? Who will decide? On what basis?

EROSION OF HUMAN RIGHTS

Since the sixties we have lived through an era of increasing respect for people who are different. These have been hard-won gains. Many of these advances have been recognized in human rights codes and legislation. However, the increased focus on the costs to society of funding social and health services, highlights how weak human rights guidelines are when the critical supports for people with disabilities are reduced or withdrawn. Human rights legislation does not prevent cutbacks. It does not prevent arbitrary decisions by institutions or care-givers or governments.

NEW WORTHINESS DEBATE

The debates about "right to die" legislation, mercy killing, the findings of the Royal Commission on New Reproductive Technologies, and our reverence for technology and medicine all reflect a belief that some lives are not worth living, or that quality of life is something that can be measured by others. Some North American jurisdictions are already publicly debating the value of providing health care to people with disabilities even if the treatment is minor and inexpensive.

CHANGING TAX LAWS AND REGULATIONS

Governments are always looking for ways to raise more money or to save money. One of the few tool boxes available to families is tax legislation that permits them to defer taxes and to set aside large sums of money without penalty for the future welfare of their loved ones with a disability. Discretionary trusts are an example. Several Canadian provinces have already attempted, without success so far, to require that the monies in the trust must be used to pay for basic services and programs.

All governments are looking at ways to tap into what has been called the largest inter-generational transfer of wealth in human history. Over $4 trillion is expected to pass from one generation to the next over the next 20 years. Will they cut back and curtail the few exemptions available to families who are simply interested in preserving some of their wealth for the future support of their son or daughter with a disability? Who knows?

LIMITATIONS OF HUMAN SERVICES

Many of you have had to contend with issues similar to these in the past. In fact, the history of the parent-based disability movement is full of unsung heroes and heroines. Mothers and fathers have, with persistence and singular initiative, created the wide array of programs and services we now take for granted. When we stop to think about it we realize the immense debt we owe to these pioneer parents.

In the ranks of parents living today are those who still remember the church basements, the bake sales, and the tremendous volunteer efforts required to gain acceptance and access for their sons and daughters in regular society. By the sixties most of these programs had become the responsibility of government. The seventies and eighties saw an escalation in their scope and number. Parent organizations grew from the tiny charitable groups that sprung up after the Second World War to the huge multi-service organizations with multi-million dollar budgets that exist today. There are now a wide range of employment, residential, social and recreational programs available in most jurisdictions to people with disabilities.

However, at the same time as these programs were expanding, parents were beginning to realize the limitations of professional human services:

• Many of these pioneer parents started to recognize that despite their years of dedication, none of the agencies they created were in a position to make a lifetime commitment to monitor and personally advocate for their children with disabilities.

• Despite the closure of institutions and the plethora of community services, their loved ones were still isolated, lonely and bored.

There were other cracks in the allure of professional services:

• Formal monitoring programs were non-existent.

• Staff turnover was high, creating instability and unpredictability.

• Control was in staff hands.

- Parents were sometimes viewed as a liability, busy-bodies in conflict with the rights of their child.
- The larger the organization, the more impersonal the services became.
- Sophisticated programs required knowledgeable advocates, which sometimes made it difficult for trusted family and friends to keep up.

New solutions for changing times

Given the general social and economic climate and the specific weaknesses surfacing within the service delivery system, parents in B.C. began searching for other solutions to their dilemma: how to safeguard the quality of their children's lives on a long-term basis.

They discovered a new form of organizing. These organizations are generally called advocacy foundations although they are referred to by various titles: continuity foundations, self-sufficiency trusts, advocacy trusts, and private guardianship corporations. The oldest, based in Seattle, Washington, has been in existence for thirty years. There are over thirty similar organizations in the United States, Australia, New Zealand and England.

Advocacy foundations are non-profit societies created for the sole purpose of providing protection and advocacy services to people who cannot represent themselves. They make a long-term commitment to the people they serve and provide future planning services to their families. We would like to introduce you to one of those organizations.

Planned Lifetime Advocacy Network (PLAN)

The Planned Lifetime Advocacy Network (PLAN) is the only Canadian organization of its kind. PLAN exists for one reason alone: to assist families to create a safe and secure future for their relatives with a disability. The founding families wanted to create an organization that would not

> We learn to do something by doing it. There is no other way.
> JOHN HOLT

make false promises, but that would find the rose in the compost. They knew there are no miracle cures (although it's a nice thought). No wonder drugs. No perfect vitamin combination. Just plain old-fashioned hard work.

They had a vision of an organization that would be there to fight and advocate for their sons and daughters long after they themselves were gone, and that would offer families everything they wanted to know about future planning, including what they were afraid to ask about. They knew from their previous experience that this meant establishing an organization that was independent of government and the service delivery system. That meant they had to be self-sufficient.

So PLAN is about:
- parents taking charge and directing the future welfare of our sons and daughters
- facing the future with open eyes
- being as clear and honest as possible about limitations and possibilities
- working together with other families
- focusing on the abilities of ourselves, our children and our neighbours
- meeting government as an equal
- accepting that we are in the same leaky rowboat together
- putting all our eggs in one basket and treating them gently
- finding roses in the compost

PLAN has five basic functions:

1. FUTURE PLANNING ADVISORY SERVICE
PLAN offers up-to-date information on all the elements of future planning. Through family visits, workshops, telephone referral, kits, newsletters, videos and personal contact, PLAN provides families with, for example:
- the latest information on preparing a will and planning an estate
- referrals to professionals sensitive to the unique issues a son or daughter with a disability presents

- advice on preserving your loved one's entitlement to government benefits
- sample will clauses

2. CREATING AND MAINTAINING A PERSONAL NETWORK

PLAN believes the best time to consolidate friends and family into a network of support is now. PLAN's future involvement in the life of a person with a disability is conditional on the existence of a Personal Network and PLAN's active involvement with the individual, the Personal Network and the family. Without this personal and intimate contact with people and their families, PLAN would not be in a position to understand, let alone advocate for, the best interests of the person with a disability.

PLAN will create and develop a Personal Network for people upon request.

3. FAMILY SUPPORT AND ADVOCACY

A common response from families associated with PLAN is the degree of support and comfort they themselves derive from developing a Personal Future Plan for their son/daughter. "This is just like the old days," is an often heard comment. PLAN's program is all based on contacts with families, starting with families. Parents co-present with professionals at all workshops. Parents make personal visits to other parents. Every family with a Personal Network is assigned a "mentor family" from the PLAN Board. Parents with Personal Networks meet regularly to share concerns and to seek advice from each other. Parents accompany each other to critical meetings as advocates.

On a broader scale, PLAN is involved with provincial and federal governments to lobby for improvements in the tax and trust laws.

4. HOUSING CONTROL – HOME OWNERSHIP

PLAN offers a home ownership advisory service through a program called the HOME Advisory Service (discussed in more detail in Step Three). Greater input and control of one's living environment is a critical factor in achieving a secure future for people with disabilities. The dream of actual home ownership with all its attendant benefits is fast becoming a reality for people with disabilities.

5. LIFETIME COMMITMENT

This is the ultimate and most fundamental function of PLAN. Families can take advantage of all the services offered by PLAN. However, if they want PLAN as an independent organization, to watch over and protect the best interests of their loved ones after they die, then they must become a full member of PLAN.

A full PLAN membership means PLAN commits to overseeing and ensuring that the future plans you have made are carried out. PLAN becomes the foundation on which you can rest all your other plans. PLAN is another check in the system of checks and balances we recommend you set up for your son and daughter.

For example full, lifetime members can expect PLAN to:
- assist and advise their trust and trustees on decisions for the benefit of their relatives
- maintain the health of their relative's Personal Network
- visit their loved one on a regular basis
- monitor the services their loved one receives
- advocate for changes that will protect or improve their relative's quality of life
- carry out any specific wishes identified by the member
- oversee the housing arrangements they have made
- respond to the unknown in a way the member would
- oversee any legal arrangements for joint decision-making that they have made
- lobby for improvements to the tax and trust system

Let your hook always be cast. In the pool where you least expect it, there will be fish.

OVID

What happens if PLAN doesn't exist in your community?

As you complete the circle of future planning described in this book, you may not be able to take advantage of PLAN's services. Don't worry. If you complete the other five steps you will have developed a far more secure future for your relative than most people ever do. A Personal Future Plan for your relative is not dependent on the existence of PLAN or on becoming a member of PLAN.

Besides, PLAN does not exist beyond British Columbia. Yet.

If PLAN doesn't exist in your community, you can find another group willing to provide the kind of backup you want for your relative. You may even want to ask one or more trusted individuals to become your unofficial backup after you are gone. Finally, you can always call PLAN. Plans are already underway to expand into other communities.

PLAN - A model for creative problem-solving by families

While PLAN is meant to assist families with their future plans, families realize the benefits of the PLAN approach right away. Families find their experiences reminiscent of their early days when the parent movement was just starting: people worked together. They did not rely on professionals or government for solutions, just each other.

PLAN believes that families are the best problem-solvers. To preserve this belief PLAN's constitution mandates a majority of the non-profit board of directors are family members. PLAN is economically self-sufficient and does not depend on government for support. Therefore PLAN can advocate and monitor without fear of reprisals.

Furthermore PLAN has only one mandate – to protect the best interests of its membership. It is not structured to diversify. The individual will not get lost in the shuffle.

Families appreciate this singular focus. For many PLAN really spells "peace of mind," now and into the future.

Achieving the complete Personal Future Plan

This workbook has presented six steps for preparing a Personal Future Plan for your loved one:

Step One Clarifying Your Vision – Clarifying your dreams, hopes and fears.

Step Two Building and Maintaining Relationships – Building a strong network of caring, committed friends and supporters.

Step Three Controlling the Home Environment – Seeking influence over the home environment.

Step Four Preparing for Decision-Making – Ensuring your son or daughter has assistance to make decisions.

Step Five Developing your Will and Estate Plan – Formalizing your intentions in legal documents.

Step Six Securing Your Plan – Appointing a monitor of your Personal Future Plan, either individuals or an organization such as PLAN.

As you have seen, each step builds on the last one. Each one on its own offers greater safety and security than many people with disabilities currently enjoy. The steps are also interrelated and taken together they offer a complete system of checks and balances. They may not be foolproof but they are thorough. And that's what's needed to replace what parents do now and to provide continuity from one generation to the next.

No one, not even those who have been involved in the future planning business for decades, is ever satisfied with their final product. There will always be tinkering and adjusting. That's natural. The difference is you will be amending a plan that is already in place. The hard work will already have been done and the basics will have been covered.

Conclusion

"Safe and Secure" is a workbook for gardeners. We have supplied you with the seeds of inspiration and information. But it is up to you to supply the rest – the planting, the weeding, the watering, and the nurturing. We are confident your shovel and hoe will dig a path into new territory. You will make the rows boldly and follow them fearfully. You will go where the rows lead. At the end you will have created your garden. In your hands your garden will have flourished. It will have become a place of security and repose.

We have supplied the seeds. You supply the love.

In concluding this book we wanted to end with some last piece that would motivate or inspire you to march right out and do everything that needs to be done. The truth is, we've already written everything we know. We've nothing left to say. No final flourish. We're still in the field ourselves, you see. Look around you. There we are – your companion gardeners. ■

John's Personal Network

John lost his speech, his ability to move, and his family when he was just ten years old. His mountain bike went out of control coming over a steep embankment and slid onto the freeway and under the wheels of a transport truck.

For the next ten years, John lived in a children's hospital, virtually alone and without visitors. Tragically, his family connections eroded over this time.

John appeared unable to communicate and seemed locked inside a fragile and unresponsive body. Fortunately, John had an ally in Darlene, who recognized John's special gifts. She met John while she was on a student placement at the hospital and she formed a deep connection with him. She visited him regularly, long after her placement ended.

John is a good-looking young man, with jet-black hair and a winning smile. His eyes compensate for his immobility. They are a window into his thoughts, feelings, soul and spirit. Expressive and penetrating, they are his sole means of communication.

Darlene and the hospital social worker recognized that John was frustrated and bored with his hospital routine. Since John does communicate his wishes using a simple yes/no signal with his eyes, they gradually developed a vision of what John wanted. He wanted to move out of the hospital and live with other men his own age. They recognized John would need a strong advocate to represent his expressed interest to government funders. As well, John would need a group of caring, committed people who would monitor the quality of service he would receive in the community.

They decided to call PLAN. They knew PLAN assisted parents to monitor the quality of life of their loved ones with disabilities. They also knew PLAN developed networks of support for people with disabilities. They wanted to know whether PLAN would perform a similar function for John, even though his family was no longer involved with him. The hospital social worker had the idea of approaching the Insurance Corporation of B.C. to finance the development of a Personal Network for John if PLAN and John were in agreement.

They were! Thus began John's new adventure. A PLAN facilitator was hired to develop his Personal Network. A new life for John began to take shape. A small group home was developed and John moved into the community with two roommates.

John's current life is unrecognizable from his previous hospital regimen. Members of the personal network visit regularly – reading with him, taking him on car rides and watching football and hockey games on TSN. One of the highlights of John's life is the regular pub visit. While John doesn't drink, he loves the atmosphere – the music, the games, the jokes, the camaraderie.

What makes these outings even more

amazing is the level of commitment that has evolved among members of the network. They operate like the sophisticated inner workings of a Swiss watch!

An outing for John is no simple matter. He has a tracheotomy and must be fed through a tube in his throat. Members of John's Personal Network have received training and are qualified to take John out on their own. Last summer two members of the network arranged their summer vacation together to go camping with John. Needless to say, this was John's first camping trip and the adventure of a lifetime.

John is no longer an anonymous statistic in a hospital environment. He is surrounded by people who care about him and have committed to a long-term relationship. Regardless of funding cuts and changing government priorities, John has a backup system. PLAN has made a lifetime commitment to advocate on John's behalf and support the maintenance of a strong Personal Network for him.

What Michael's mother did

Michael was 50 when his mother died. The house he had lived in with her for 28 years was sold. What could his mother have done to protect Michael from the trauma of finding a new place to live?

In fact, Michael's mother had planned the future very carefully. Through her will she had directed her house to be sold. The proceeds were to be put into a discretionary trust for Michael. The house was her only asset and had to be sold to create the financial security she wanted for Michael. She had located a reputable trust company sensitive to her wishes for Michael. She was convinced the trust officer of the local credit union would spend the trust monies in Michael's best interests. Besides, she had a backup. A family friend had suggested Planned Lifetime Advocacy Network (PLAN).

Michael's mother became a full member of PLAN. That meant she consulted with PLAN on every aspect of her future planning. Through PLAN she met other parents facing the same question: "What will happen to my son when I die ?" Two years before her death she also asked PLAN to facilitate a Personal Network for Michael, so that he would have a circle of friends. Michael's mother knew she didn't have much time left. She wanted the comfort of seeing Michael surrounded by people who cared about him. She shared her hopes and fears with them while she still could.

Being a full member of PLAN also meant that Michael's mother could direct PLAN through her will:

- to provide advice to the trustee;
- to maintain Michael's circle of friends;
- to monitor his services and health care; and
- to stay in regular touch with Michael lifelong.

Moving out of the family home wasn't traumatic for Michael. He, his mom and his circle of friends had prepared for two years. The PLAN representative helped Michael find his new place. His circle of friends borrowed the truck, moved his possessions, built his bookcases and hung his curtains. Even the trust officer got into the act, holding onto the family photographs and eventually placing them into the albums with Michael after the move.

That's the backup Michael's mother had in mind when she signed a full PLAN membership contract.

Worksheet 7

YOUR SUMMARY CHECKLIST

I have completed all the following documents:

☐   A "family portrait" of my loved one.

☐   My letter to the future, clarifying my wishes.

☐   A list of my loved one's documents: birth certificate, social insurance card, health care card, etc.

☐   An up-to-date will that reflects my current wishes.

☐   A description of the purpose of the discretionary trust.

☐   A up-to-date list of my major assets and where they are kept (insurance policies, bank accounts, stocks, mutual funds etc.).

and

☐   I have stored all these documents in a safe place.

☐   My executor knows where these documents are kept.

Resources

Materials

STEP ONE

Marsha Forest, Jack Pearpoint and John O'Brien
Planning Alternate Tomorrows with Hope (PATH)
Toronto: Inclusion Press, 1994
The folks at PLAN like this one a lot. It's an exciting planning process, providing a good way of stepping out of the day-to-day and allowing your heart and mind to soar. Excellent structure for strategic and future planning.

Pat Beeman, George Ducharme and Beth Mount
"Dare to Dream: An Analysis of the Conditions Leading to Personal Change for People with Disabilities"

"Person-Centred Development: A Journey in Learning to Listen to People with Disabilities"
Available through Communitas Inc., 730 Main Street, Manchester, CT. 06040, U.S.A. Phone: 203 645-6976

Polly Berends
Whole Child, Whole Parent
New York: Harper Collins 1987
A good read for parents of all ages.

Stephen R. Covey
The Seven Habits of Highly Effective People
New York: Fireside, 1989
An inspiration to all those who want to put their external and internal houses in order. A best-seller for years and deservedly so.

STEP TWO

Claude Whitmyer, editor
In the Company of Others
New York: Jeremy Tarcher, 1993
This is the best compilation of writing on the art of community development and building community connections.

Margery Williams
The Velveteen Rabbit - How Toys Become Real
In bookstores everywhere.

Jack Pearpoint
From Behind The Piano - The Building of Judith Snow's Unique Circle of Friends
Toronto: Inclusion Press, 1990
This is the book to read if you want to learn more about an amazing human being and one of PLAN's two great guardian angels.

Judith Snow
What's Really Worth Doing and How To Do It - A Book for People Who Love Someone Labelled Disabled
Toronto: Inclusion Press, 1994
Words of wisdom and inspiration from one of the wisest.

Best Boy, a film by Ira Wohl
This one won an academy award several years back. A true story in which the director filmed the process of his cousin, a middle-aged man with a disability, leaving home. You can find it at most video stores or libraries.

Dave Wetherow, editor
The Whole Community Catalogue, 1992
Invaluable tips, articles, stories and leads for anyone interested in building relationships and community connections for people with disabilities.
Phone Dave at 604 248-2531 to order copies.

Pat Beeman, George Ducharme and Beth Mount
"One Candle Power — Building Bridges into Community Life for People with Disabilities"

"What Are We Learning About Circles of Support?"
Available through Communitas Inc., 730 Main Street, Manchester, CT. 06040, U.S.A. Phone: 203 645-6976

And Then Came John –
The Story of John McGough
A video by Telesis Productions, Mendocino, California
This remains one of our favorites. A true story of an artistic man and the love that emanates from his connections in the community. Available from PLAN.

A Guide to Personal Networks, a PLAN publication
Available from PLAN.

Marc Pilisak and Susan Hillier Parks
The Healing Web — Social Networks and Human Survival
University Press of New England, 1986
This book will give you all the theory behind the importance of social networks. A classic in our opinion. A must read for anyone who wants to dig a bit deeper.

"The Common Thread"
4638 Centre Avenue, Pittsburgh, PA. 15213, U.S.A.
A first quality newsletter. We subscribe and you may want to as well.

STEP THREE

John O'Brien
"Down Stairs That Are Never Your Own: Supporting People with Developmental Disabilities in Their Own Homes"
Syracuse University, Centre on Human Policy, 1991. Available from Responsive Systems Associates, 58 Willowick Drive, Lithonia, GA 30038. Tel: 404 487-9785
Good overview of alternatives to group homes and the conceptual shift that will be required in order to achieve widespread home ownership or rental accommodation for people with disabilities.

*Housing Issues and Options for
People with Disabilities*
Vancouver: Social Planning Research
Council of B.C. 1992
A look at B.C. home ownership for
people with disabilities. Available
through the PLAN office.
PLAN also has various reports and
briefing papers on this emerging
approach.

STEP FOUR

Tony Appolini and Thomas Cooke, eds.
A New Look at Guardianship
Baltimore: Paul H. Brookes Publishing
Co. Inc., 1984
An excellent overview on U.S. responses
to assisting people make decisions.

David Schwartz
*Crossing The River: Creating a Conceptual
Revolution in Community and Disability*
Cambridge, Mass.: Brookline Books,
1992
The best description from an American
point of view on the new way of
thinking, or the paradigm shift, in social
services for people with disabilities.

*How Can We Help? A New Look at
Guardianship, Interdependence, Substitute
Decision Making and Guardianship in B.C.*
1992
This book formed the background to the
new B.C. Guardianship legislation.
Available from the Community Coalition.
See address on p. 149.

Robert F. Murphy
The Body Silent
New York: W.W. Norton, 1990
There is an abundance of books written
about and by people with disabilities.
Without a doubt this is one of the best.
An anthropologist writes about his own
gradual experience of becoming a person
with a disability and what keeps him safe
and maintains his quality of life.

Advocacy Without Burnout
Produced by the Advocacy Access
Project of the B.C. Coalition of People
with Disabilities. See address on p. 149.
A good overview of the advocacy
process. Well worth getting.

STEP FIVE:

*Wills and Estates: Planning for Parents and
Families of Persons with a Disability*
A brochure prepared by the People's
Law School. Call 604 331-5400 for a
copy. Copies are also available at PLAN.

Robert Kerr
The Only Retirement Guide You'll Ever Need
Toronto: Penguin Books, Financial
Times of Canada, 1994
We agree. It is complete and
comprehensive. Well worth the price.

Will and Estate Kit
Produced and distributed by PLAN.

Stephen G. Wong
Wills for British Columbia
Vancouver: Self-Counsel Press, 1993
A handy and readable reference.

Elmo A. Petterle
*Getting Your Affairs in Order – Make Life
Easier for Those You Leave Behind*
California: Shelter Publications, 1993
An American look at the dilemma we all
face.

STEP SIX

John McKnight
The Careless Society
New York: Basic Books, 1995
This represents the best of John's
writing. Inspired by the CBC radio
series, "Community and Its
Counterfeits." John is the second of
PLAN's two great guardian angels.

John McKnight and John Kretzmann
*Building Communities from the Inside Out: a
Path Towards Finding and Mobilizing a
Community's Assets*
Center for Urban Affairs and Policy
Research, Northwestern University,
Chicago, Illinois, 60208, U.S.A.
We continue to model our work at
PLAN on John McKnight's analysis and
insights. This book is available for sale at
PLAN's office.

Organizations

Planned Lifetime Advocacy Network
104 - 3790 Canada Way
Burnaby B.C. V5G 1G4
604 439-9566

B.C. Association for Community Living
300 - 30 East 6th Ave.
Vancouver, B.C. V5T 4P4
604 875-1119
The federation for people with mental handicaps is now forty years old and still going strong.

B.C. Coalition for People with Disabilities
204 - 456 West Broadway,
Vancouver, B.C. V5Y 1R3
604 875-0188
The premier advocacy organization representing people throughout the disability community.

Community Legal Assistance Society
800 - 1281 West Georgia Street
Vancouver, B.C. V6E 3Y2
604 685-3425
Provides free legal advice and representation on issues affecting people with disabilities. They have always been there when needed.

Community Coalition for the Implementation of Adult Guardianship Legislation
204 - 456 West Broadway
Vancouver, B.C. V5Y 1R3
604 875-0188
The coalition is one of the most powerful examples of the strength that comes when the community works together to achieve law reform. A strong and powerful grassroots coalition.

Family Support Institute
300 - 30 East 6th Avenue
Vancouver, B.C. V5T 4P4
604 875-1119
Canada's first family support organization for families who have sons and daughters with disabilities.

HOME Advisory Service
c/o 104 - 3790 Canada Way, Burnaby,
B.C. V5G 1G4
604 439-9566
Advice and referral offered to families who are interested in obtaining a home for their son/daughter with a disability.

Vela Housing Society
c/o 300 - 30 East 6th Avenue
Vancouver, B.C. V5T 4P4
604 875-1119
This organization concentrates exclusively on developing micro boards for people with disabilities.